Do You Mean Me, Lord?

Do You Mean Me, Lord?

*The Call
to the Ordained Ministry*

Robert G. Cox

The Westminster Press
Philadelphia

First edition

Published by The Westminster Press®
Philadelphia, Pennsylvania

PRINTED IN THE UNITED STATES OF AMERICA

9 8 7 6 5 4 3 2 1

Library of Congress Cataloging in Publication Data

Cox, Robert G. (Robert George), 1951–
  Do you mean me, Lord?

  Bibliography: p.
  1. Clergy—Appointment, call, and election.
2. Clergy—Office. I. Title.
BV4011.4.C69 1985   253′.2   85-8785
ISBN 0-664-24668-0 (pbk.)

To my sons—

Joshua Christian Cox
who knows something the rest of us don't
and
Ian Christopher George Cox
who dispenses sunshine wherever he goes

Contents

Acknowledgments

Writing a book of this nature is a humbling experience in more ways than one. Only with fear and trepidation do you offer advice to those the Almighty calls!

Much to my relief and, I am sure, your inspiration, I have relied on the thoughts of many different people. I wish to acknowledge my interdependence and gratitude to my parishioners who have so richly ministered to me at the Presbyterian Church of the Covenant, Denver, Colorado; the Presbyterian Church of the Lakes, Orlando, Florida; and the St. Paul's Presbyterian Church of Detroit, Michigan. My hat is also off to those authors whom I have quoted, including Rev. Donald K. Campbell; Dr. Howard L. Rice, my doctoral adviser; Rev. Robert and Mary Garment, Dr. William Arnold, and Dr. Wayne Oates, whose anecdotes I used; candidates I interviewed; scholars and counselors who were sought out; my clergy colleagues; seminary professors at whose feet I sat; and my supportive family. The hard work of typing the manuscript has been accomplished by my past and present secretaries, who were all of great assistance at one stage or another in the process: Janet Fethke, Ann Hill, Jim Fanning, Marie Butler, Vi Miller, Carol Baluk, and Jane Hutchins.

I wish to offer my thanks not only to all the special people in my life who have exhibited what the love of God is all about but also to those I have been privileged to know who have been promoted from the Kingdom on Earth to the Church Triumphant!

1

Do I Have a Call? or
Does God Even Know My Number?

A fourteen-year-old boy walked into George's study one day and said, "I've received a call." George said that was nice and asked him who he had received a call from. "No, you don't understand," said this young man. "I have received a call from God."

George was a little taken aback by this but, being very interested in this young man, asked him how his call came about.

"Well, a girl in my ninth-grade history class asked me to go to church with her on Christmas Eve. We sat up in the balcony, and when the minister began to pray, she reached over and held my hand. And I've never felt like that before!"

How mysterious and awesome are the words "a call." They conjure up images of burning bushes, lightning strikes, booming voices. In this book I hope to explore with you the meaning of a call and some of its implications. Together we will be going on a spiritual pilgrimage that may be one of the great religious quests of your life. Whenever you go on a pilgrimage, you must know that the itinerary cannot be set, nor can you be aware of the outcome of the journey. Let me assure you, though, that a true pilgrim will always come back richer.

So loose thy shoes from off thy feet as we move into the realm where heaven and earth brush.

As you contemplate your possible call to the ordained ministry, first be aware that you will really be moving through four distinct calls. The great theologian H. Richard Niebuhr is the one who identified these different calls (p. 46)*: (1) the Call to Be a Christian, (2) the Secret Call, (3) the Providential Call, and (4) the Ecclesiastical Call.

With shoes in hand, let us strike out.

The Call to Be a Christian: The Call of Calls

The word "call" literally means summons, and God summons each of us to do a specific task in our walk through life. The common calling we all have, the reason we mysteriously ended up on planet earth, is to follow in the footsteps of a Palestinian Jew, a carpenter from Nazareth, the Son of God and the Savior of the world. Whatever else we may happen to be and do in this life is secondary to our calling to serve Jesus the Christ.

As followers of Christ, we have joined the saints who carried the torch of faith down through the ages and passed it on to us, so that we, in turn, may pass it on to those who will come after us. A Christian is to engage in ministry and use her or his talents so that God's love may be more than a nice theory. Our common ministry to which every Christian has been called is absolutely, positively, and beyond any shadow of a doubt the most important divine calling we shall ever receive. Everyone is summoned to serve as a minister for Christ. Martin Luther said it best when he referred to "all" of us as the "priesthood of all believers."

The church, for whatever reason, has never understood this concept very well. The one we call Reverend is only one minister in a congregation full of ministers. You are a minister. (I'll bet you thought it would take more schooling.)

If you have not come to terms with your "call to be a Christian," the rest of this book will be of little value. This paramount call is the foundation upon which the rest of the mortar and bricks are laid.

The key word is "obedience." Jesus apparently loved the water, for he seemed to spend much time near it. The fishermen mending nets were "summoned" by Christ, and in obedience they followed. Matthew, also called Levi, a tax collector, the scum of the earth, was called and obediently followed. Simon the Zealot,

---

*Full references for all citations may be found in the Bibliography.

a political revolutionary, responded in obedience. Christ's follow-ers formed a microcosm of humanity. What an unlikely and motley band was originally gathered together! You can be sure Jesus had to sleep between some of them to make sure that one of them didn't awake in the night to find his own blood spilling upon the ground. They had one thing in common—their love and devotion to Jesus.

Others heard but did not follow the summons. The rich young man who had it all but couldn't give it all was unable to accept the call. Others had graves to dig. The cost, the risk, the commit-ment was too high a price to pay. Some laid it on the line, others didn't.

Dietrich Bonhoeffer, a great and a promising German theolo-gian, wrote in *The Cost of Discipleship* about the difference between cheap and costly grace. Cheap grace is accepting the love and the forgiveness of God without commitment to disciple-ship, without understanding the cross, and without total devotion to Christ. Costly grace, on the other hand, is the call to follow our Lord. "Above all, it is *costly* because it cost God the life of His Son: 'ye were bought at a price,' and what has cost God much cannot be cheap for us. Above all, it is *grace* because God did not reckon His Son too dear a price to pay for our life, but delivered Him up for us" (p. 48).

In a personal way, Bonhoeffer came to know the cost of following Christ and the weight of the cross. Before the beginning of the Second World War, he was in the United States giving theological lectures. His many friends pleaded with him to stay in America. The situation in his homeland was rapidly deteriorat-ing, but he took one of the last ships back to Germany.

Because of his spiritual persuasion, which was in opposition to what was happening under the Nazi regime and Hitler's de-monic influence, he joined the Confessing Church. On a bright Monday in April 1943, Bonhoeffer was arrested by the Gestapo. It was then that he wrote what were later collected and published as his *Letters and Papers from Prison*.

Fellow prisoners and guards alike were deeply moved by his contagious sense of joy and abiding faith. His ministry did not come to an end inside his prison cell. An English officer who was imprisoned with Bonhoeffer said, "He was one of the very few men I have ever met to whom his God was real and close" (*Letters and Papers from Prison*, p. 11). On Sunday, April 8, 1945, during a worship service for fellow prisoners, the S.S. guards told him to get his things ready. The following day, at the age of thirty-nine, a few days before the arrival of the Allied Army, Dietrich Bonhoeffer was hanged.

Christ issues the call and invites us to take his yoke upon us. In the assurance that Jesus shoulders our lot, we are freed to take the risk as we dare to live a life in obedience to the Lord Jesus Christ. "My yoke is easy, and my burden is light."

"The call to be a Christian" is the paramount call. We have made far too much of the distinction between laity and clergy; we all have been called to minister.

Faith, like love, demands expression. Each Christian must determine how she or he must express devotion to Christ. An ordained minister is no more or less holy than is any other Christian.

A friend of mine who is an attorney once remarked that if we placed all the lawyers in the state of Colorado end to end, we would probably be better off. Some people would say the same thing about preachers.

So if all are called to minister, why are there ministers? The church has found it beneficial to set aside persons to perform special tasks. Thus, an "ordained" minister is one who because of the privilege of special training is entrusted with the function of preaching the Word and administering the Sacraments. The professional minister assists the ministers.

I have gone to a great deal of trouble in this book never to refer to a minister or the ministry when what is meant is an ordained minister or the work of a professional minister. May my subtlety not be lost. It is not a matter of whether or not you have been called to minister. It is a matter of ultimate importance, though, how you are going to work out your ministry in obedience to Jesus Christ.

The Secret Call: The Inner Urgency

Agatha Christie pieces together a mystery by dropping clues, and it isn't until the end of the book that who dun it is revealed.

If you knew the ending at the start, you would see that everything fits nicely into place. In the consideration of a secret call, look at all the clues God has deposited within your heart and life.

In that you are already a minister, which was formally accomplished at the time of baptism/confirmation, you may feel called to a specific work within the church. It is apparent that you must have some inner urge to consider the vocation of an ordained minister, or you are really hard up for some good reading material. (Vocation is from a Latin word that means a summons or an invitation.)

God's private call to an individual can often be difficult to discern if not downright troublesome. A feeling of an inner calling may persist, with emotional highs and lows, for several years before the time when the call either dissolves or is solidified. Inner turmoil is not uncharacteristic of a person struggling with a consideration of the vocation of an ordained minister.

The secret call comes in many ways at many different times and to many different people. The laity, who still believe they have no ministry, will often have an almost unhealthy interest in how someone was "called" to the ordained ministry, the same way in which people stare at a two-headed cow or a bad accident.

An inner sense of call may come to a person in a subtle way that might best be described as a growing awareness, or the call may come in a highly dramatic fashion. Or, it may come as a combination of a growing awareness and one or more mountain-top experiences. Even when a call appears to be a bolt out of the blue, there has often been some prior groundwork leading up to the experience. There appears to be about an even split between those who emphasize a growing awareness and those who have had a highly dramatic experience. Either way, you are in good company.

The one thing you can say for sure about all the secret calls is that each one is unique. In all the interviews I have conducted with people, there was never a faint resemblance between one call and the next. As God made us unique, so he approaches us. This is indeed a private affair between the Almighty and you, and in that order.

Therefore, the most important action you can take is to wear out your knees. There can be no excuse for not going directly to the source of the problem. Ask, seek, and even bang on God's door and ask him the meaning of all this. If you need to learn how to rant and rave a little, the writers of the psalms will be of great assistance.

Live with your call and allow it to develop or dissipate. A person may be definite one day, indefinite the next, so it is often the long view that is of the most help.

Come to know and appreciate how God has called the biblical characters and be amazed at the various types of saints, sinners, swingers, and shysters who have been called to serve God in a special way.

Talk to your local pastor or any other ordained minister with whom you identify. The individual whom people struggling with a call found most helpful by far was their pastor. Parents are usually seen as supportive while the pastor normally proves helpful. There are exceptions to this rule of thumb. Women, in particular, do not always find the local pastor helpful. It is vitally important to seek out the counsel and prayers of an ordained minister with whom you identify.

The wilderness is a powerful biblical image. The Israelites struggled with their faithfulness to God in the desert after escaping from bondage in Egypt. Jesus, after his baptism, was driven out into the wilderness to wrestle with the meaning of his life and vocation. The inner call is like a stint in the desert as you struggle with the meaning of God in your life and how you must respond to your particular summons. Many people have been surprised at the message discovered in the wide-open places. Do not minimize or short-circuit the soul-searching process as you attempt to hear the voice from beyond and within.

I knew one young man who happened to be darn near perfect. If it wasn't for the fact that he was just a great guy, he would be downright nauseating. He became interested in the ordained ministry. He was outgoing and caring; he enjoyed speaking and did it well; he was a leader at school and very involved in his church; and he was intelligent and related well to people. I had no doubt that if he chose the ordained ministry he would be a terrific professional minister, except for one problem. He felt no inner urgency. Someone who cannot discover this sense of inner persuasion at some point along the way should be ordained. An interest in the ordained ministry without an inner call just does not cut it. (It may be just as well, since there is no reason to give the rest of us an inferiority complex.)

The inner call you may be experiencing may remain vague even after you begin seminary, which for some becomes the final proving ground. For others, the call is already "fixed."

Women are often less sure about their calls prior to seminary because they have had so few role models. In many instances, women talk about how their sense of calling really came together after the first semester at school.

The call is not, and should not be seen as, a lifetime commitment to a specific type of ministry. Just as God calls people into the ordained ministry, our Lord also calls people out of it to perform ministry in other ways. Your inner call is not necessarily a forever call. The church has been slow to realize this fact. This is evident, particularly in those denominations in which a person becomes ordained under the normal rules of church order but can only lay aside the ordained office under the rules of church discipline. The church, particularly in our day and age, needs to reconsider the concept of a call as being a forever commitment.

The inner call may still be troubling you and it is important to maintain a certain amount of tension, which only you can work out with God. However, keep your spyglass in place as we do further investigation into this awesome mystery.

The Providential Call: Getting It Out of the Head and Into the Being

Taking an afternoon siesta in my college dorm room one day, I awoke to the sound of what seemed to be somebody taking a sledgehammer to the top of my door. It couldn't be human since people knock on the center of the door rather than at the top. As the door continued to shake at its hinges, I began to feel like I was in a King Kong movie. I yelled, "Come in," more out of fear than hospitality.

Joe entered the room. He is probably the tallest and most muscular human being I have ever been within six feet of, the kind of person who, when he scratched an itch, his T-shirt pleaded for mercy. "Your roommate said I could borrow his tape."

"Take it," I offered immediately. I think I heard myself add, "Take anything you want."

As you may have guessed, Joe was on our football team. Oddly enough, Joe was only on the team for one season before the coach retired him. He also retired Joe's jersey, since it would have taken two people to fill it. The problem was that Joe was no doubt one of the clumsiest of all God's creatures. The whole incident convinced me of how dumb a football coach we had. To my mind, it would have been worth giving Joe a full scholarship just to have him suit up and sit on the bench, staring at the other team while crushing Pepsi cans on his forehead.

Some people do not dabble in minor vices, but that is not my case. I am addicted to caffeine. During my distinguished coffee-drinking career, I have also discovered I spill a lot. To put it another way, if you needed a lobotomy, you probably wouldn't want me as a surgeon.

Joe will never be a ballet star, and I will never operate on anything more than a well-done hamburger.

We are talking about talent.

Your inner sense of call must be balanced against the abilities you possess. You may or may not be particularly gifted in conjunction with the demands of the ordained ministry, while still realizing that no one is fully adequate for the task.

Chapters 2 and 3 will deal with some of the personal and professional qualities found compatible with ordained ministry. Measure yourself against those factors which it seems desirable to possess.

Volunteer your time to a local church and really get your feet wet. If you have never been in the water, it is hard to know if swimming will come natural and be enjoyable.

Ask your local pastor if you can shadow her or him. Even if you make your pastor a little neurotic in the process, you may come to learn a bit more about the professional ministry and what it requires.

Seek out the counsel of your denominational officials, because there are clearly defined ways in which a minister becomes an ordained minister. There are committees established for the sole purpose of helping people like you.

If you are considering the ordained ministry, you need to examine your own heart, motivations, interests, talents, and intelligence. You also need to have your head examined. Most denominations require that you go through a series of intensive psychological, vocational, and aptitude tests with a qualified counselor. This is an invaluable way of helping to answer the big question, Do I have what it takes?

Occasionally, the vocational counselor will find someone who has severe emotional problems. Sometimes people will focus their neuroses in their religious faith and mistake a deep problem or an unmet need for a call to the professional ministry.

Certain things about you only you can ever truly know. Other things a good counselor can point out. A vocational counselor cannot tell you if you have a call, but going through the process adds one more experience to help in making your decision.

The most creative time to see the vocational counselor is when your call is still in its formative stage. I have never met an individual who has gone through this experience who regretted it or failed to learn something special about herself or himself. Normally it is a positive affirmation of your gifts, with just enough concern thrown in to guarantee a place in the human race.

It is essential that your secret call and your providential call are in correspondence with one another. Line up what is happening within you with what your talents are. You may feel the strongest inner urgency to enter the professional ministry, but if the necessary abilities are not present, it would be better to consider fulfilling your call in another way.

Every time Christ called someone, it always involved a move. Feet always get in the act. Peter left the boat on shore and Matthew left his 1040 forms. Let us venture on now to the final leg of our journey.

The Ecclesiastical or "I Made It" Call

Where would I be if I were . . . a poet without a pen . . . an actress without a stage . . . a singer without a song . . . a fisherman without a sea . . . a shepherd without a flock?

Ecclesiastical means of the church. The church as represented by your denomination ordains a minister to serve in local churches and in other professional ministries.

Graduating from seminary does not make you an ordained minister. It makes you a graduate of a theological institution.

Thus, the fourth and final test of your call is in being recognized by your denomination as qualified to assume the duties of the ordained minister. Once you have satisfied all your denominational requirements and have been called to serve in a recognized ministry of the church, then you will be ordained.

Let me wave a couple of red flags at this point.

First, be sure to follow carefully all the particular rules and regulations concerning ordination in your denomination. You would be surprised at how many supposedly intelligent divinity students fail to take a required class or fail to be under care of a certain part of the church for the required period of time.

Second, this is one heck of a time to find out that you really have not been called to the professional ministry. There are certain people who are to be gatekeepers for candidates. They are to let in some and not others. Opening a door for some and closing it for others is a difficult task. Gatekeepers in the candidacy process include local pastors who make recommendations, local churches who sponsor candidates, and the denominational candidate committees.

The keepers of the door are assisted by what they know of you, your vocational tests, your academic performance, and your sense of call. Sometimes gatekeepers are too kind and not kind enough at the same time.

We do not do a great service to our candidates when we let them go through all the procedures and schooling and then confront them with the reality that no one wants to hire them. Or, worse, they do receive a call and the church suffers as a result, and the ordained ministers involved never fully recover from the experience.

I have been very impressed by some candidate committees who have loved their candidates so much that they were even willing to say no from time to time. Other committees never say no to any candidates, short of their being Jack—or Judy—the Ripper.

It is my hope and prayer for you that your gatekeepers will have the church's and your best interests at heart, for it is much easier to have a gate gently closed at the beginning than to have a door slammed in your face at the end of the process.

The question still remains, "Do I have a call, or does God even know my number?" Most assuredly you have a call to ministry, as does every other member of the body of Christ. And maybe you have a call to the ordained ministry. We can't be sure of that until the date of ordination is set.

You can, though, be well assured that God does have your number.

The God who reigns in glory from everlasting unto everlasting is the same God who came to us in Jesus Christ and walks beside us. Spend a few moments with your divine guide before you take another step into the unknown which looms before everyone who attempts to be faithful to Jesus' call, *"Follow me."*

2

The Ideal Ordained Minister, or
The Art of Aqua-Ambulation

Besides the traditional abilities of being able to walk on water (aqua-ambulation) and part seas, what are some of the personal characteristics which a minister to ministers needs to possess?

Imagine going into a roomful of people where everyone is a stranger to you. Look around and attempt to find the person you would want to be your pastor—if you needed a pastor. You would probably find someone who is really concerned about you, who is willing to listen to your concerns, and one with whom you can identify. In other words, you would find an individual who has good relational skills.

"In the vocation we call ministry," writes Murdo Macdonald (p. 23), "a certain level of intelligence is indispensable, but in the long run, it is not as important as a capacity for establishing a warm living contact with people."

It is not my intention in this chapter to build for you the bionic minister. It is impossible to relate to you the stuffing that goes into filling up a capable ordained minister. Uniqueness is one of God's gifts, and this needs to be evident within the leadership of the church. This is vividly illustrated by the fact that pastors with vastly different personalities and different strengths can follow one another in the same church and still be effective. Keep this caution in mind, while we identify some general personal characteristics that have been found to be especially compatible for someone interested in being a professional minister to possess, and then we will examine personal qualities that may be considered detrimental.

For help with this task, we must turn to the exhaustive study regarding the "Readiness for Ministry" project as it is summarized in Schuller, Strommen, and Brekke's volume *Ministry in America*. This extensive study is a look at what laity and clergy value in those who are leaving seminary and joining the ranks of the ordained ministry.

The value that was rated the highest is "an open affirming style. A style of ministry that reflects a minister who is positive, open, flexible; who behaves responsibly to persons as well as to tasks" (p. 25).

> It is a theme of ministry in which the priest or minister not only "works at further development of pastoral skills" but also "helps others see the best in people" and "shows a good mixture of seriousness and joy." It includes both an approach to ministry functions in which a minister "does not avoid tasks of ministry he or she does not enjoy" and an approach to life in which he or she maintains "personal integrity despite pressures to compromise." The theme portrays style in the foreground and function in the background. The factor's high rating indicates that, while the expectation of ministry or priesthood in North America includes competence in functions, it is also highly sensitive to the character and spirit of the person who carries out these functions (p. 30).

The ministry is all bound up with persons and personal relationships. God summons ordinary people to take care of extraordinary tasks. Who we are as persons, how we relate, and what we believe have a major impact upon how well our task is accomplished. James McCutcheon wrote (p. 128), "I remember, as a young minister who was still insecure in his personal faith, coming away from the graveside of a teen-aged boy I had just buried. The father and I walked to the family car. Neither of us said anything. But just before disappearing inside, the man turned and said: 'I don't know if I believe everything you said back there. But it means more to me than you can imagine for me to know that you believe it.'"

The "Readiness for Ministry" project also lists (pp. 32–39): "Caring for Persons Under Stress, Congregational Leadership, Theologian in Life and Thought, and Ministry from Personal Commitment to Faith" to be important. Don Campbell, then staff associate in the office of professional development of the former Presbyterian Church U.S., wrote a paper titled *Enlistment of*

Candidates in a Day of Job Scarcity, in which he identifies as needed pastoral qualities such things as "flexibility," "intelligence," "courage," "selflessness," and "people skills." The Vocation Agency's Office of Counseling Resources of the former United Presbyterian Church cites "tolerance for ambiguity," "realism in self-appraisal," "resiliency" and a "willingness to be a fool for Christ" (p. 6) as helpful traits for the ordained minister. Roy W. Fairchild wrote a paper for the same agency on *Discerning Your Call and Your Gifts for Ministry,* in which he stated (p. 7): "The professional minister must tolerate long hours, misunderstandings, idealizations, tensions, and irrational love and hostility. Unless he or she has a solid sense of identity, an ability to form true friendships, and empathy, and a tolerance for ambiguity (all crucial gifts), perhaps another avenue for vocation should be considered."

One of the important personal characteristics is good health. Great physical and emotional demands come into play every day of a pastor's life. In a calling that is so draining, it is important for a person to be able to meet the task with energy and dedication. Someone who is not well will never be able to fulfill a call.

On the other side of the ledger is the negative picture. These are considered to be "Disqualifying personal and behavioral characteristics: Self-protecting ministry, avoiding intimacy and repelling people by a critical, demeaning, and insensitive attitude, undisciplined living, irresponsibility to the congregation, professional immaturity, pursuit of personal advantage, and secular lifestyle" (Schuller et al., eds., *Ministry in America,* p. 49).

Again, you may recognize in the foregoing list a very high emphasis on the person of the professional minister rather than on professional competence. In the professional ministry, it is at times difficult, if not impossible, to separate the person from the profession. It is a life-style where relational skills and personal traits have an unbelievably high value. This may be unfair and often is, but it is a reality, and one you may have to live with. Recognize it. Other ministers do expect, and maybe have a right to expect, much in the way of personal qualities from their minister of ministers.

In the process of a call to the ordained ministry and as one works toward it, a transformation often occurs. As part of one's personal characteristics, one begins to feel and to relate as an ordained minister. There is a shift away from "I am playing the part of a pastor," to "I am, as a person, a pastor. This is me." The vocational identity and the selfhood, at least to an extent, become fused.

It may be helpful to use the image of an ordained minister as a fool or a clown for Christ. The mask we wear is symbolic of God's presence, and it must be something that is authentic for us. As David Switzer in *Pastor, Preacher, Person* says (p. 18), "Quite apart from one's own being as a person, the pastor is perceived by others as being the physical representation . . . of the reality of God." Within the most personal areas of being, an ordained minister must live as one who is convinced of the power of the Living Lord. If Christ appeared foolish in the eyes of the world, then we are also to put on clown makeup as we attempt to represent and embody the reality of our Lord's presence in this world. Our calling must show in our lives or, as Switzer poignantly states, "We cannot lead a person to what we are not" (p. 22).

Maybe this is why, within mainline Protestant churches, which have had shrinking memberships, there is an urgent concern for stronger and better pastors. For in studies, it has been shown that the healthy or growing congregation has vital pastoral leadership (e.g., Calian, p. 7).

As part of the Peace Corps training, there was a twenty-four-hour survival stint alone in the jungle. One volunteer, according to William Sloane Coffin (p. 195), came back visibly shaken: "You know, as soon as I found some running water and got my hammock slung where I figured no tarantula would get me, I knew I'd be all right. But then it suddenly hit me: in the next twenty-four hours I'd have to pay a call on myself and I wasn't sure I'd find anyone at home."

If there is ever a profession in which you need to know yourself, it is the vocation of a professional clergyperson. "One's personality is on the line at every turn," says Edgar M. Grider (p. 25). "Understandably, an extremely high level of anxiety must be tolerated by the young minister just starting out. Possibilities of disapproval, rejection, personal failure are anxiously tested almost daily." Grider goes on to point out that even our very reason for being, and our call to be professional ministers, is called into question.

So who is the ideal ordained minister? I don't know! I do know that God calls some marvelous and very unusual people to serve as the servants to others. I do know that God takes some rather raw ability and transforms individuals to carry the Word. I do agree with Dr. Frank Williams that God calls into "ministry bright and capable people, who believe that God in Christ has something very important to do in this world and are committed to being a part of it."

As has already been made evident, the personal characteristics and the role expectations of an ordained minister are often inseparable. In the next chapter, it will be important to give consideration to the positive and negative elements of the role of an ordained minister because "our professional status . . . is determined by the competence with which our loving is done, not just to the degree to which we love" (Switzer, p. 25).

3

The Role of an Ordained Minister, or I'd Rather Feed Hogs

I wished Don the best and told him I would miss him. Don was leaving seminary and going back to work on his family's hog farm in the Midwest. Don was halfway through his seminary experience and had completed his Greek and Hebrew requirements; in many ways it was all downhill until graduation.

Don was a genuine person, whom I came to know briefly in a counseling class. He had the academic skills and what I thought to be the good relational qualities needed to be a very special professional minister.

Don and his wife would drive every weekend to a small rural church and spend the weekend ministering to those church folk. Coming from a farming environment, he knew well the kind of community he was dealing with. Those good church folk, though, ·were too much for him in regard to their constant criticisms, and he decided to leave his calling to the pastoral ministry. The ministry lost a good potential ordained minister when it lost Don. As he was getting into his packed car, after we shook hands and said good-bye, he said, "I understand hogs, but I sure don't understand people."

Don came to know early what many of us come to realize later: the strains and stresses which others bring to us or we bring upon ourselves within the pastoral ministry are enough to make a saint do some pretty strange things.

As we combine the personal qualifications for ordained ministry with the role expectation for clergy, we again are aware of how much God expects of us mortal creatures. As Grider says (p. 16):

I can think of no more anxiety-prone profession, no line of work where anxiety is more pervasive or more acute than the ministry (except perhaps steelworkers or window washers on skyscrapers!). Anxiety is our constant companion in the ministry; and we are peculiarly susceptible to it. For the anxieties of people tend to get focused in their religion, more particularly on the minister in the local congregation.

The job of an ordained minister is not an easy one, nor are some of the role expectations fair. It is the express desire of this author to point out some of the negative factors about the ordained ministry, not to discourage anyone but to be realistic. Like Reinhold Niebuhr in *Leaves from the Notebook of a Tamed Cynic* (p. xii), I "make no apology for being critical of what I love."

The ordained minister is one who is honored by some and ridiculed by others. The image of clergy can be anything from Father Mulcahy of M*A*S*H, a nice but inept fellow, to the Reverend Mr. Dimmesdale in *The Scarlet Letter*, a cowardly hypocrite.

Daniel Jenkins (p. 7) tells of a poster in England, toward the end of the 1930s, which called for everyone to register due to the war emergency. The sign read:

> ALL PERSONS IN THE ABOVE AGE GROUPS
> ARE REQUIRED TO REGISTER
> FOR THE NATIONAL SERVICE
> EXCEPT LUNATICS, THE BLIND,
> AND MINISTERS OF RELIGION

Professional ministers are often regarded as a third sex, and we are often flattered when a parishioner tells us, "You're not a typical minister." Whatever vocation we might choose, we know that people will view us with a certain amount of prejudice, but for an ordained minister it can be a double standard. The statement of the British author G. K. Chesterton speaks of this: "'People pay ministers to be good, to show the rest of us it doesn't pay to be good'" (quoted in Calian, p. 75). Jan C. Walker in *Why Me, Lord?* (p. 20) recalls the words of a school administrator: "'For years I thought the minister was a pious ass who walked four feet off the ground.'" "Within the ministry," writes David Jacobsen, "there is a high degree of discontent, confusion, and questioning about the role" (p. 18).

As will become evident, the role of an ordained minister can be very helpful when understood and used correctly. At this point, it is safe to say that it is a very difficult problem to untangle the self from the role.

It is only fair to state that there is major concern over the large number of pastors dropping out of the parish. As in every age, there appears to be major confusion over the mission of the church and the role of the ordained clergy. Some would even go so far as to inquire whether or not someone should be encouraged and affirmed in the pursuit of the ordained ministry.

A recent Gallup Poll as written up in the *Journal of Psychology and Theology* (9[3]:244), reported that "one third of all pastors were found to ponder the implications of leaving what they thought would be a life work." In an article in *The Washington Post* titled "Clergy Burnout: When Stress, Overwork Overwhelm the Spirit," the Rev. Kenneth "Burke, a 1958 graduate of a Southern Baptist seminary, said he believes his class has had an extremely high burnout rate, with several members committing suicide, and others giving up the ministry to sell used cars or pump gas. His class president gave up his collar to lay bricks."

In some ways I think it is only now coming to light how many pastors are suffering some of the unhealthy slings and arrows of the pastorate. When one major denomination did a study on stress in the ordained ministry, it discovered, according to the *Journal of Psychology and Theology* (9[3]:245), that "three of four ministers reported feeling stress severe enough to cause depression, anguish, anger, fear and alienation." This problem is apparently not restricted to Protestant clergy; one New Jersey rabbi was reportedly so alarmed by the rising rate of dropout, divorce, ulcers, heart attacks, and suicide among his fellow rabbis that he took steps to establish a counseling program.

From a study by the United Church of Christ came a book by Gerald Jud and others titled *Ex-Pastors: Why Men Leave the Parish Ministry*. The report concluded that there was really no single factor which led the professional minister to leave the parish. However, it did conclude (p. 51) that "the fact that the ministry is an extremely demanding job is reflected in the primacy of reason one, a sense of personal and professional inadequacy, as well as in the incidence of personal illness or breakdown." The other reasons for leaving, in priority listing, included: "unable to relocate when necessary, problems of wife and children, opportunity to put training and skill to fullest use, personal illness or breakdown, dissatisfaction with parish work, lack of church's spiritual growth and relevance was stultifying, divorce or separation, money problems, more attractive job opportunity, and other reasons" (p. 50).

As you can tell, this study was conducted only on men because there were not enough women clergy leaving the parish to make a study. It probably will not be too many years before we read about "why women leave the parish ministry."

There are some helpful suggestions pastors are using to deal with the high level of stress, which appears to be part of the ordained ministry. I hope that the more this problem is recognized by the laity and the clergy, the more steps will be taken to reduce it.

Nine to Five

The ordained minister is on call twenty-four hours a day, seven days a week. Within this life and vocation, an ordained minister in a local church is called upon to perform various functions effectively. The number and variety of these duties can be both challenging and frustrating, as you may see by following your pastor around.

There is no such thing as a typical day in the life of a pastor. Virtually every day brings new demands upon an ordained minister in what is required on a personal and professional level. Calling upon the sick in the hospital, counseling a couple in trouble, conducting the funeral of a young cancer victim, writing a newsletter, attending meetings, establishing an outreach to the needy, and shuffling a lot of ecclesiastical paper may be all bound up in a pastor's day. A pastor is always involved in the lives of people. I cannot tell you how many times I have picked up the phone to find someone in tears at the other end of the line.

Even the most visible act of a pastor, preaching, is often more of a complicated business than what it might appear. For in the act of preaching, a pastor needs to be a theologian, a biblical scholar, a writer, a commentator, an editor, a humorist, a prophet, a public speaker, and a translator. It is imperative that we be competent at what we do. We go to medical doctors, assuming that they know something about the human body. In the same sense people look to pastors to know about God and the workings of the kingdom of God as represented in the church community.

The future promises to bring even a greater need for pastors that are not only capable in dealing with the traditional disciplines of theology but also skilled in new dimensions of life. Whether it be a theological consideration of test-tube babies or a consideration of the ethical implications of a computer, the local ordained minister will need to bring his or her thoughts and prayers to bear upon the world of tomorrow.

The great demands placed upon an ordained minister are what often cause major stress and frustration. And so much of what a pastor does cannot be seen in a visible way.

Even with all its frustration and difficulties, I believe with David Jacobsen that the ordained ministry is a special privilege because "no profession offers richer opportunity for person-to-person contact" (p. 42). An ordained minister is given many keys and is able to unlock many doors. Who else is regularly received into the homes of people? Who else has the privilege to watch and pray with a dying patient? Who else is called upon to join couples in marriage in the presence of God? Who else is called in times of personal turmoil? Who else has the privilege of breaking the bread or pouring the wine? Who else is charged to speak and to preach and to stand on the front line in causes of social concern? As Carnegie Samuel Calian, President of Pittsburgh Theological Seminary, so correctly states (p. 47), "This is our vocation: to bear witness in the marketplace to the reality and presence of God in all dimensions of life." As in no other walk of life, ordained ministers have the privilege and opportunity to engage others at close quarters.

William Sloane Coffin, the preaching minister at the Riverside Church in New York City, originally felt that the church was indifferent to social need. However, after listening to professors and visiting storefront churches in Harlem during a prospective students' weekend at a seminary, his mind was changed. For he records in his autobiography (p. 88) that Bill Webber, then a pastor in one of these storefront churches, sealed his decision to enter seminary with the words that "ministers who had the courage of their convictions and knew what they were about had greater freedom to say and do what they wanted than good people in any other vocation."

Words are inadequate to express that special feeling a pastor has for her or his people. It is a unique and special attachment. The deep caring between pastor and people is a two-way street that a pastor is richly rewarded for traveling. Very often people express the special feeling they hold for "their" pastor in subtle yet important ways. At other times, people are highly demonstrative of their love and concern.

Ordained ministers get special boosts along the way when they know a sermon was meaningful to someone or when a prayer was able to give expression to a deep chord in another's life. How marvelous it is for a pastor to be able to lie down at night after a good day, and almost imagine the words "well done, good and faithful servant," and remember that the promise of a new day will provide yet another opportunity for ministry.

The joyful tasks of ministry bring compensation and satisfaction not even imaginable in other walks of life. Whenever pastors and their families move to a new community, they have a host of people ready to befriend them. The pastor is an important member of a community and is able to exercise leadership and influence. Most of all, though, the pastor is fortunate because of the privilege of working full-time for Christ. And how can there be a more joyful task than sharing in word and deed the good news that God is love and that we can come to know God in Jesus Christ?

Fulfilling a calling by God through the office of the ordained ministry can be one of the most demanding and exciting areas of service. It is a vocation that will use every fiber of one's personal being and every ounce of one's professional expertise. There is perhaps no other calling that will so richly help develop a person into the human being he or she was intended to be.

Authentic Ministry

It is important to come to an understanding of the real role of the ordained minister. Some of the strange perceptions of ordained ministers have been discussed; it would take many pages to complete such an investigation. James D. Glasse made an interesting assessment of this situation when he said in his book *Profession: Minister* (p. 19) that a minister is like a politician because the "minister is made to look like something he (she) is not in order to clarify who he (she) is."

One of the ways in which we discover how to minister is by trying on the roles of how we think we ought to act. This concept is vividly exemplified by Edgar Grider during his first hospital visit (p. 77):

> While a seminary student, I was called to administer last rites to a ninety-two-year-old woman of Catholic persuasion. She had been in a coma for weeks. It was my first hospital visit and, being Presbyterian, I had almost borrowed a classmate's clerical collar, but didn't.
>
> I entered the hospital room and saw a shriveled, inanimate little form on the bed; only the machines attached to her body gave forth any sounds. The old woman's middle-aged daughter stood to greet me with a smile.
>
> The daughter was my mother's age! My face smiled stiffly while my eyes squinted nervously. I reached for my pocket Bible as I desperately tried to piece together the words to a suitable prayer. Almost tripping over a tube, I approached the bed with such somber bearing and grave face that it would have made a funeral director proud!
>
> "I'm so hungry I could eat a horse! You want a cup of coffee?" The daughter's bright tone pierced the fog like sunshine; and she led me gently down to the cafeteria. We talked: she of her husband and three children (I reminded her of her middle son!) and of her mother, who had led a full and enjoyable life.
>
> Slowly I relaxed and began to share something of myself: my background, my hopes for the ministry, my interest in sports.
>
> Twenty minutes later she suggested that we go upstairs and have a prayer; we did, both of us, holding hands at her mother's side. Although I never saw her again and can't remember her name, I owe a great deal to that woman!

As you can gather, hiding behind the supposed role of an ordained minister can be damaging to authentic ministry. One of the great concerns for anyone working toward the ordained ministry is attempting to deal with the proper and improper roles of a professional minister. James N. McCutcheon brings this into focus in *The Pastoral Ministry* (p. 128):

> Not so very long ago, the parish minister was safely encased in a universal stereotype. He always was male, wore dark suits, black shoes, and a conservative tie. He didn't smoke, drink, play cards, take his wife dancing, or go to the movies. . . . The black suit and the pious whine have been removed. The real parson is now right out front for everyone to see. And for better or worse, the parish minister is going to make it, or not make it, on what he or she as a person actually is.

It is a tragic fact that there are people who are attracted to some of the more artificial roles of an ordained minister and not to the more authentic vocation that might lie beyond those roles. It is a special challenge to adjust the roles and to utilize their symbolic power in such a way that authentic ministry can really take place. "We need to use the symbolic power of our role, but without hiding behind it or exploiting people with it," according to David Switzer (p. 23).

In many instances the role of an ordained minister and what it represents need not be rejected but, rather, used in such a way that people are led to God's redeeming presence. A dying patient may find the presence of an ordained minister invaluable. For that patient, at that time, the role of that ordained minister as a representative of God is what is important. Although we need to get away from certain false stereotypes of the ordained ministry, it is important that the baby is not thrown out with the bathwater.

There are many models for ministry, and certainly they may be considered legitimate as having a foundation in the life of Christ. However, the most profound of these, to my mind, and the one which comes closest to being representative of the life of Christ is the role of a suffering servant. It is thus my contention that a call to ministry may be a call to great joy and happiness, but a call to ministry is also a call to a painful task. "If there is no pain," writes David Jacobsen (p. 34), "there is less than a ministry."

As we look at the life of Christ, we see a man who was called to perform a difficult task. Indeed Christ "was despised and rejected by men; a man of sorrows, and acquainted with grief"

(Isaiah 53:3a). Jesus was a person who had real role problems, because he never seemed to be doing what people expected of him. He was more interested in fulfilling his calling to ministry.

The reality of the world about us is often pain, sadness, and tragedy. It is into these situations that we are called to go. David Jacobsen says it well (p. 86):

> The fact of life is that we still live in a world where love and joy and pain and birth and death are real. Persons put on these facts of life daily, and we are called to minister to persons through our own humanity—through our own love and joy and pain and death.

A very real part of the call into the ordained ministry is realizing that who we are as individuals needs to be brought to bear on the lives of others. Our own sense of humanity must be brought with us as we attempt to minister to another's pain. It is a very risky business getting involved in the life of another in a personal way, but that is exactly the call of an ordained minister. When student nurses are taught not to get too personally involved in the lives of their patients, this may be good advice for them. However, this is exactly opposite to the role and calling of the ministry. It is in the engagement of our personal being and of our professional skills that authentic ministry really takes place.

Henri Nouwen, in his marvelous book *The Wounded Healer* (p. 23), offers us the realization that an ordained minister cannot be aloof but must remain vulnerable, even if that open posture causes great personal suffering.

> Who can save a child from a burning house without the risk of being hurt by the flames? Who can listen to a story of loneliness and despair without taking the risk of experiencing similar pains in his own heart and even losing his precious peace of mind? In short: "Who can take away suffering without entering it?"

As Christ was called to be a suffering servant, so also we who minister in his name are called to be his "wounded healers." "Ministry 'happens' most authentically in the midst of suffering and ambiguity. One's own human predicament forms part of the response of ministry." We cannot be mere spectators in the pain which others bring to us, but we must be willing to share in their pain and respond to their pain as healers, who also have been wounded, for "only those who have been wounded may speak of healing" (Schuller et al., eds., *Ministry in America*, p. 8). Our common humanity in the service of our Lord will require us to throw our arms around a fellow sufferer. The words of our Lord Jesus Christ tell us how to minister: "Greater love has no man than this, that a man lay down his life for his friends" (John 15:13).

The call to ministry is not a call to a safe task. It is a daily call, though, to put all that we are and all that we possess on the line for the sake of others, in the name of Christ.

4

The Ministry and the Family, or Warning! This Profession Could Be Hazardous to Your Marriage

There is a bad joke going around these days that "all the Roman Catholic priests I know are getting married and all the Protestant ministers I know are getting divorced." There seems to be a certain amount of truth in that statement.

As we have already mentioned, the professional ministry is more a way of life than a job. Thus, the boundaries of home and church often become so interwoven that they become indistinguishable. Again, we need to be aware of the interpersonal nature of the professional ministry, as well as our interpersonal relationships with our families. All these networks will sometimes become very confused, and we will fail to differentiate between our relationships appropriately.

When the lines become too fuzzy, tension and stress experienced at home or at church are bound to affect each other. Obviously, taking out frustration on a spouse because of a disagreement with a parishioner will not endear you to your wife or husband. In a similar sense, family problems can unfairly color relationships with church members. For everyone's benefit, it is important for the professional minister to distinguish between home and church and to learn how to deal constructively with conflict in an appropriate manner.

For many of us, the person we turn to for pastoral help is our spouse, who will generally offer us the appropriate dose of encouragement, strength, and love. It is critical when the husband/ wife relationship gets out of kilter. Ordained ministers often become drained in the process of being overworked and overexposed to people, their problems, and their crises. In order to survive this emotional and physical exhaustion, we often will draw from the emotional well of our spouse. So often, though, we draw off the energy but never give anything back in return. Is it any wonder that they complain about getting the crumbs? Is it any wonder that they ask, "When is it my turn?"

I am speaking about the traditional ministry of male clergy and the difficult roles wives have to play. (There are so little data about how the clergywoman's husband is faring that it is impossible even to speculate.) There are various ways in which the wife of an ordained minister will cope with being "the minister's wife." She may accept the role wholeheartedly, with all the responsibilities that go with being an unpaid and unsung assistant pastor. There are even books on seminary shelves, mostly collecting dust, on how to be a dutiful minister's wife. Although this secondary role for some may still be legitimate, I am not at all sure it is healthy for either the wife or the church.

At the other end of the spectrum, we find ordained ministers' wives who have had it with the church and are openly hostile to the whole business. These women often retreat entirely from the life of the church.

Maybe in between these two positions lies the healthiest way of handling the situation. The solution for an ordained minister's wife is to "be yourself." Ruth Truman, an ordained minister's wife, learned the hard way how important this is. "As a girl growing up in a Methodist parsonage," says Truman (p. 7), "I had vowed I would never, no never, marry a minister." Well, as you can guess, she did, and her views of the whole business are recorded in her hilarious book *An Underground Manual for Ministers' Wives*. First she reaches for the perfection which others look for in "the minister's wife" (p. 17).

> If you're not careful, you will begin to think you are supposed to be perfect. At housekeeping, child-rearing, entertaining, church work, spiritual living—wife exemplar! Of course, you know that you are clumsy; you always say the wrong thing at the wrong time; you've scarcely learned to pray in private, let alone in public; you buy all drip-dry clothes because you can't iron a thing without scorching it; and you've just begun to figure out your husband. When he preached

on the text "take up your cross and follow me," you didn't figure he was speaking to you personally!

Ruth Truman, along with many other wives of ordained ministers, has learned the hard way how wrong it is to attempt to live up to the expectations of what a minister's wife is supposed to be, say, and do. She offers the following advice (p. 17): "You need to examine and separate what you do because you want to from the things you do because you think you are supposed to. People outside have a neat word for this condition in life. It's called 'hypocrisy.' The New Testament expressly forbids it. But how we ignore that injunction."

The women's movement has done a great deal for many women, including the wives of ordained ministers. In a loving, caring relationship, it is essential that each partner be able to grow into the fullest human being possible. This is why our Creator gave us so many gifts and so much potential. "Witnessing maximum completeness of one's mate will bring fulfillment and satisfaction to each partner," writes Calian (pp. 64–65).

Working outside the home has been a great help to many wives of the ordained clergy, as they gain a sense of identity outside the church. In addition, this has become an economic necessity in many cases. It is essential that we attempt to continue to educate congregations when it comes to expectations of spouses.

David and Vera Mace have written a book entitled *What's Happening to Clergy Marriages?* They have done extensive study and research into this important area. It is interesting that every topic of concern was a mixed blessing, with positive and negative elements about it. For example (p. 45), "the high expectation of the congregation can be viewed as either judgment or challenge. The burdens of the work are compensated for by the fruits that it may yield. The joy of caring for people in distress leads unavoidably to emotional exhaustion. The pressures applied by congregational demands are at least partially mitigated by nurturing support and individual deeds of kindness."

According to the Maces' investigation, wives of ordained ministers are having more trouble coping with their lot than their husbands. Although the Maces' work seems to be representative of the more traditional clergy marriages, they certainly point (p.

41) to some deep needs and concerns raised by the wives of clergy.

> Taking these responses as a whole, we get a rather disturbing picture of the clergy wife carrying a heavy load. Denied adequate time for maintaining the intimate relationship with her husband, she often feels lonely and frustrated. Add to this a great deal of confusion about what exactly the congregation expects of her. Then there is the feeling of uncertainty about developing friendships outside the church; and, if she feels she ought to take an outside job or wants to do so, she must consider how far her husband can be counted on to share the homemaking duties. Add all this together, and we begin to understand why she has so much difficulty handling her negative emotions.

Although it is often easier to point out the difficult aspects of the marriage of an ordained minister and spouse, it is also important to consider the positive benefits. Many couples consider it a joint adventure or a shared vocation as they attempt to help others in need. It is obviously a vocation that allows for a great deal of joint participation. It is not the kind of job where one goes off to some mysterious place to do work that is totally unknown to the family. The sense of doing something meaningful within God's vineyard is an important aspect, when the concept of fulfillment is considered. With the difficulties that so many couples are experiencing in marriage and with the breakdown of families, a pastor's healthy marriage can be a powerful and beautiful statement to others.

If there is one thing that is important in the whole consideration of clergy marriages, it has to lie in the sense of mutual support. A wife or a husband (or a potential wife or a potential husband) who has no investment in a spouse's calling to the ministry is in for some very serious trouble. If a spouse is not openly supportive of the partner entering the ordained ministry, one should not do it.

Love on Campus

Hugging, kissing, and squeezing are allowed on most seminary campuses. Beyond that highly useful bit of information, there does not seem to be much sophisticated information about how couples fare on a seminary campus. As far as I can determine, the marriage rate and the divorce rate are probably close to the national average, which is not all that encouraging.

A word of caution may be in order. A couple may come to a seminary campus with less than a stable marriage and hope to have their problems magically cured. They probably will be greatly disappointed. If someone is using seminary as a way to resolve marital discord, the chances of succeeding are pretty slim.

Harry Barrow, the former Director of Admissions for Columbia Theological Seminary, has done research on students who were married for a relatively short time before entering seminary. The three main problems these married couples had to deal with were financial strain, emotional strain, and quality time together. According to Barrow, the issue of finances kept coming up time and time again, which may be partially symptomatic of the times in which we live. Very often the number-two problem, emotional strain, was tied in with the tight financial dilemma. It is important for a seminary couple to carefully map out their financial situation in order to lessen this concern as much as possible.

It is my firm contention that more time and energy need to be spent in support of the spouses of seminary students. The students' spouses need some help and guidance in consideration of what may await them, once they enter into a local congregation. Classes and support groups ought to be set up especially for them, as part of the regular responsibility of a seminary.

Those students who are coming directly from college into seminary are often adjusting to three different major life transitions. Many students marry before or during their seminary career, many are moving from late adolescence into adulthood, and many are moving from the secular life into the clerical life. All these changes are affecting not only the married seminary student but also the spouse. Major adjustments and times of life transitions are not known for their smoothness, and again seminaries need to offer a major support network to help their students move through these times. As Vera and David Mace have stated (p. 31), "The seminary which fails to understand these adjustments, and does not provide all possible support and help to the couple, must be regarded as delinquent."

In a marriage, whether it is a young one or one in which many years have been invested, there is always the danger of one partner outgrowing the other. When one of them is a seminary student, that one is bound to be doing some growing which may not be shared by the partner. Although I do not agree with David and Vera Mace concerning their reservations about Clinical Pastoral Education, I can appreciate what they mean when they say (p. 131) that "when one partner in a marriage is involved in a program that produces significant personal growth and change, with the other partner uninvolved or excluded, alienation within the relationship is a frequent and sometimes fatal consequence."

Seminary students have many resources and many people available to them. It is my hope that every seminary will also take equally seriously its commitment to the support and development of their students' spouses. In this way, marriages of seminary students and of ordained ministers will be strengthened, and commitment to the ministry of marriage enhanced.

Role reversal may also be an issue, but probably not as big a one today as it was in former days. In those days, the husband came to study and the wife came and got a job. The wife bringing home the bacon and the husband frying it up was often a bit more than some traditional egos could stand. Unless things have progressed further than I imagine, there may still be some twinges of "this isn't the way it is supposed to be." In this instance, as in almost all cases, talking helps.

Maybe the more dramatic role reversal today is in being a husband of a seminary student. This role, which remains largely undefined, could also be a concern as the husband pursues his own vocation and need for identity. There remain a lot of unanswered questions about how this new dimension is working itself out within the personal lives of people.

Clergy couples, where both wife and husband are in training or ordained, are also a relatively new phenomenon. Again, there is not much substantial evidence about how they are doing. Some studies suggest that this has caused many divorces; other studies show that the marriage and divorce rates are average but that the divorce of a clergy couple is simply more noticed. The arrangements, both practical and philosophical, can be complicated, frustrating, and beautiful when both the husband and wife hope to be or are called Reverend.

Religious and Single

"Catholic priests fight to marry," writes Laile Bartlett (p. 120), "Protestant clergy have to. Both are stuck with a phony image and counsel of perfection: one of celibacy, the other of marriage." It is indeed ironic that most Protestant churches want their pastors to be married, even though these same churches often place very difficult demands on the pastor's spouse.

There is sometimes a difficult element for a single female or a single male ordained minister in relating to others in the church. Carol, an ordained minister, has problems in relating with some men who feel "there's got to be a woman under all the Sunday clerical garb." She, like male ordained ministers who are single, is sometimes accused of being gay. And Carol, like some single male clergy, is pressured to get married. However, when she tried to share this concern in a talk with her parishioners one evening at a church dinner, she was "totally misunderstood," because she quipped, " 'What I really need is a wife.' " (Quoted in the Proctors' *Women in the Pulpit,* pp. 11, 12.)

Guppies in the Bowl

It is sometimes difficult being a kid in a pastor's family, as Ruth Truman recalls (p. 16):

When I was a little girl, I used to get very aggravated because somebody would always die just when our family planned to go somewhere. This feeling stayed with me well into the early years of our marriage, and even though my head told me people didn't deliberately get sick or have trouble just as we were leaving on that long-awaited vacation, my emotions would still get tangled up with the little girl inside me who just wanted to climb in the car and drive away.

Although there are probably worse places to be reared, children are bound to be affected by the fact that Mom or Dad is a pastor. There are a lot of assumptions about P.K.s (preacher's kids) or the more modern T.O. (theological offspring), but like most generalizations they don't hold much water. It is even fair to say that generally the children of ordained ministers do rather well in life, and many of them also become members of the cloth.

Even with the assurance that it is not a crime against your children to be a pastor, it is important to remember that they are in a little different position from that of most children. In addition, the amount of time you spend with them is often less than it should be. It is pretty tough trying to explain to your daughter why you cannot go to her ballet performance or to a mother-daughter banquet or explain to your son why you cannot go on the father-and-son campout. If you choose to be an ordained pastor, don't fall into the dangerous trap of forgetting about your calling and commitment as a spouse and a parent.

An ordained colleague of mine was going out after a quick supper to one more meeting in an endless sea of meetings. His three-year-old daughter led him by one finger toward the door, gave him a kiss, and in all seriousness said, "It was good to see you again, Daddy. Come back and see us again, when you get a chance." If an ordained minister fails to properly love and care for those she or he lives with and sleeps with, that person's God-given ministry has missed the mark.

5

College as a Time of Preparation, or Not What I Had in Mind

Hoover Rupert in his column in the *Presbyterian Outlook* was telling about a friend of his, Jim Crane, who is a cartoonist. In this particular column entitled "Not What I Had in Mind" (162[7]: 9), Rupert writes about confusion of motives. He does this by referring to one of Crane's cartoons:

> He portrays a person, obviously a college student, who is grappling with the meaning of his own life and what it would be for him to serve. In the series of four pictures, the character says, "Use me, Lord use me—I'll go anywhere, do anything—suffer abject poverty, make any sacrifice, even martyrdom." Then, in the final picture he is simply sitting there, looking depressed. And he says, "Well, studying wasn't exactly what I had in mind."

The advice offered in this chapter will not be of much help if you have already completed your college course of study. However, if you are beginning college or are partway through college, this information might suggest a few things for you to consider.

During the college experience, an individual heading for seminary needs to stretch and grow as a human being. Pursuing a liberal arts degree of one sort or another will be your best preparation. The one suggestion most often given to pre-seminary students is "Don't major in religion." The reason is that you will need to have a broad scope of understanding in which to support your graduate study in religion. I realize this may seem a bit peculiar to you. After all, if someone wants to get a master's degree in physics, that person must have a basic degree in the same field. The same, however, does not hold true for seminary.

In addition to the need to be exposed to the other humanities, majoring in religion at the college level is not ultimately the best use of your time. Since you will probably not be able to bypass any seminary courses, and because the seminary classes will be so much more intense, your college major in religion will not get you much farther down the road. By all means, take some religion classes as electives, but majoring in religion is probably not the best route.

Many different areas within the humanities will be of real help to you in seminary and within the professional ministry. Psychology will be important (reaching into the scientific realm) as well as the related areas of sociology and social work. Speech and theater can be of great value in the development of your speaking and creative ability. English and creative writing skills will surely come in handy, as well as a general knowledge of history. Although many people enter seminary from a variety of different college backgrounds, the liberal arts disciplines will be the ones that will provide the best foundation for you.

Let us consider your college experience from another perspective. Realizing some of the realities of the present job market (refer to chapter 12), you may want to consider having another career possibility to go along with the professional ministry. This may be in order to do a tentmaking ministry (working a secular job in addition to church work), or it may simply offer you an option, if you ever need one. It would be ideal to have a separate identifiable skill, such as teaching certification, coming out of college.

If the mission field is a possibility for you, you might want to consider majoring in agriculture and learning a foreign language. If you wish to become a bilingual pastor for a Hispanic congregation, majoring in Spanish would be a logical first step. If you desire to be an outstanding preacher, majoring in speech or theater may be your first choice. If someday you would like to be a church administrator, stepping outside the liberal arts realm for some business classes may very well be in order. If you wish to become a religious writer, journalism may be the way to go. These are simply suggestions, in order to jog some creative possibilities for you and in order to suggest that you intentionally prepare for your seminary experience and your work as an ordained minister.

So much of the problem with attempting to give direction to a pre-seminary student in college is that advice appears to be premature. Very often people will change their minds within seminary about exactly where they are headed. Someone who feels called to the pastoral ministry will take a counseling class and decide to specialize in pastoral counseling. Another person who wanted to be a prison chaplain may discover a love for work in a local church. Part of the job of both college and seminary students who are bound for ordination is to remain open to the possibilities that God may offer. Remember, though, God expects you to be very much involved in the process.

If you are uncertain as to your future in the ordained ministry, it is better to take a course of study that you enjoy and that will be of benefit to you, regardless of whether or not you attend seminary. People enter seminary with majors that include everything from religion to engineering to nursing to photography. If the seminary of your choice is worried about your academic background, you may be required to take some remedial work, which will be arranged for you, as part of your course of study.

Languages may be something to consider before seminary. In some denominations, such as the Presbyterian, Greek and Hebrew are required. You may wish to take these on the college level rather than in seminary. German is seemingly the language of theologians, and if scholarship is in your future, this will be your first choice for a modern language. If you are more practically oriented, Spanish may be of greater value.

The Association of Theological Schools has a brief statement on preparation for seminary students. A student, according to the A.T.S., should be capable of independent thought, should be capable of effective communication, and should be capable of research. Of all the seminary catalogs I have perused, I have found only one school that offers a suggestion as to a pre-seminary course of study, and it is in vague terms.

The reality of the situation is that there is not one college concentration that will magically prepare you for seminary. You must contemplate what will be of the most benefit to you as a unique individual as you possibly prepare for the ordained ministry. If you know seminary is in your future, you are very fortunate. Intentionally prepare yourself for seminary by developing into the fullest and most well-rounded human being that you can possibly be.

Your classroom work at college is of great importance and will provide the platform for your seminary career. It is important to learn how to study, to be able to do research, and to gain the necessary skills with which to pursue a graduate degree.

As important as your studies are for your preparation for seminary, what you do outside the classroom is equally important. This is the time to get involved in worthwhile groups and projects. Attempt to discover life in all of its many facets and get to know all kinds of different people and how to relate to them. This would also be an ideal time to devote some spare hours to assisting the college chaplain or helping at a local church.

During one summer of your college career, you may want to consider working with a Christian ministry in the National Parks. College students who are heading for seminary are often accepted. If you are hired for a summer, you will be placed in a park job or a park-related job in one of the national parks. You earn an income through your secular job. Also, you will lead worship services or help lead worship services in a campground or other park setting for a nondenominational congregation of vacationers. It could be a great way to spend a summer!

The Value of Dropping Out

Making a life decision is normally difficult, but it is extremely far-reaching and profound when you are considering an all-out commitment to the ordained ministry. Some would suggest that we very often make these life decisions at times in our lives when we are not really in the best position to do so. William Perry, for instance, in his book *Orchestrating Your Career*, says (p. 25), "Your field of work should complement your talents and interests. Unfortunately, at the time of life most people choose their field of work, few know their talents, interests, or even the career options available to them."

A college student is in that stage in life we refer to as young adulthood or what developmental psychologists would refer to as late adolescence. Erik Erikson and the other great developmental psychologists suggest that it is important for a person to have a psychological moratorium or a lying-fallow period, before one begins to narrow down life choices, which would certainly include a decision to enter the professional ministry.

It may be appropriate to define this psychological moratorium or fallow period as the need to have space, prior to making an all-out decision. It is important to have a period in which you have the freedom to think, and dream, and contemplate. This time can be essential in regard to your identity formation. "An Abraham Lincoln could sit with uninterrupted thoughts, free day after day to turn and look into himself," writes Wayne Oates (pp. 22–23). "Goethe, failing in his studies at Leipzig, said that he could do nothing except love, suffer, dream, loaf and let his spirit grow. Darwin failed in medicine and embarked on a sea trip aboard the Beagle. 'His eyes were freed for the unexplored details of nature.'"

College and seminary often provide settings for this psychological moratorium, and yet, with all the pressures associated with an academic setting, this may not be the best location for a fallow period. In the past, and to a certain extent today, young adults went into the Army or joined the Peace Corps as a way of gaining a period of psychological moratorium. The fallow time for Martin Luther was when he was learning to become a priest in a monastery and was required to adjust to a totally new way of life, with a great deal of regulation and regimentation built into it. (See Erik Erikson, *Young Man Luther*, p. 132.)

The young adult years are often the interval between your past and the future that awaits you. It is important to be able to link your past and your future together. In religious terms, it is essential for you to be able to weld together your heritage and your pilgrimage. For most of us, college will encourage us to untie some of our continuity with our past. However, this interruption of the connection with our past should be balanced by a reconnection with a new future. It is at this time that the fallow period becomes important.

In order for you to develop, it may be important to have a time when you "drop out" (not necessarily in a literal way), in order to learn about yourself without fretting about what you want to become. If you can do this creatively, you can gain a good perspective on the tension that exists between your identity and your proposed vocation. This is the time when you need to learn about what is most meaningful to you.

Although many college students who are planning to become ordained ministers move directly from college into seminary with only a summer break, I am not so sure this is the ideal. You may want to consider a year in between to have a full-fledged, unadulterated fallow period in your life. This might be a time when you enter the business world, which could be of great benefit in relating to your parishioners later in life. Or this might be the time when you work on an oil tanker. Or this might be the time when you conduct rafting trips down the Colorado River.

Your commitment to the life of an ordained minister may be helped along by taking some time out before you enter seminary. This period in your life may give you the freedom to roam around inside yourself and in the world, before you are thrust into the hectic life of a seminary student. Although you may feel the need to get on with things, I hope you will at least consider the possibility of calling a special kind of "time out" in your life as you search for all those special treasures and adventures which only seem to be readily available at the young adult stage of life.

Our Lord went out into the wilderness in order to be alone with his thoughts, to contemplate and to pray. Maybe we could define this period as our Lord's psychological moratorium. This was a time when he fasted and expanded the horizons of his senses. This forty-day experience in the desert was the preparation for his public ministry. If Christ needed this period in his life, it may also be very helpful for us who attempt to minister in his name.

The Value of Reaching Out

If you are convinced of or are seriously contemplating accepting a call to the ordained ministry, this is the time to make contact with your pastor and with your denomination. There are people who can help you in this process, and the earlier they know of your interest, the greater the help they can offer. It is certainly no disgrace to become interested in the vocation of the ordained ministry and then decide it is not what you are after in life. This happens to many, many, many people!

This may also be the ideal time to head toward a career counseling center, which can help you assess your mental, personal, and vocational aptitude for the ordained ministry. This is a time to reach out to God and to others who can share with you in your pilgrimage toward what God would have you do in this life.

6

The Ordained Ministry as a Second Career, or You Are Going to Do What!?

Jim had become very successful in the business world, and his family had reached that stage in life where everything was secure and comfortable. It was the so-called good life, but then God came with a call for Jim to enter the ordained ministry.

Jim, Sally, and their elementary-school children left the nice home, the cars, and the boat and headed for seminary. The family was deeply troubled about what this would do to their relationships and family life. Jim had always worked and Sally had always taken care of the children. Now Jim would be in school and would take care of the children, while Sally would enter the paid work force.

To everyone's delight, Jim discovered that he loved taking care of the children and Sally discovered that she loved working outside the home. What appeared to be a potentially disastrous arrangement turned into the most meaningful of situations.

An individual who is thirty or older might be classified in the category of a second-career student. It is amazing to look over the list of first vocations of older seminarians. The list ranges from pharmacists to undercover narcotics agents, from Christian education directors to homemakers, from lawyers to contractors, and from musicians to dentists.

In certain aspects, an older candidate will often have more at stake or at least different concerns when considering the ordained ministry. One of the dimensions is time. The candidate who enters seminary at age thirty-six will not graduate until the age of thirty-nine. This investment of three years of time needs to be addressed.

The major concerns for older candidates can be described by two words: family and finances. Giving up a secure job and uprooting a family is by no means an easy decision. Trauma is bound to strike. The adjustment problems will need to be carefully considered and addressed by everyone involved in the experience. With the reality of the general low pay of pastors and the uncertainty of the job market, there simply is no guarantee that the financial part of the investment will really balance out. There are some students who, upon graduation or soon after, return to their first careers.

In at least one instance, the loss of a job precipitated the call into ministry for an older individual. This person had been wrestling with the meaning of a call in his life but had not really done anything about it until the air controllers strike, and the subsequent loss of his job, forced him to examine more seriously the inner sense of God calling him into the ordained ministry. In a number of instances, there often appears to be a major life occurrence that often forces one to examine a sense of calling.

According to Dr. Arlo D. Duba, former Director of Admissions at Princeton Theological Seminary and the present academic dean at Dubuque Theological Seminary, there is a great distinction between older men and older women entering seminary. In the cases of the older men, according to Duba, about 75 percent of them felt some sense of call in high school or college but did not respond to it at the time. It has been his experience that in most cases the wives of older students were very much involved in the decision to enter seminary and are very supportive and very encouraging of their husbands.

There are few helpful data available on how marriage of second-career male students weathers the radical change to student and seminary life. However, one tentative study by Brightman and Mollette points to some very encouraging conclusions. In their sampling and research, the authors discovered that older male seminary students and their wives perceived their relationships to have improved since entering seminary. The research is written up in the *Journal of Pastoral Care* (31[1]:58):

While all areas of the relationship are perceived to have improved by both groups, husbands rate consensus on goals as having improved the most, while wives ranked verbal communication as most improved. There is virtually complete agreement on improvement in the areas of relations with extended family and friends, and sexual relations. This is indeed a beneficial state of affairs when husbands report that wives agree with them more, and wives report that husbands talk with them more.

The most striking phenomenon concerning older women students, according to Duba, is that more than half of the women over age thirty have been recently divorced. The older, divorced women students, who are often single heads of households, are common to many seminaries; this is in no way unique to Princeton. It is apparent that, at least for some older students, seminary serves as a reorientation to a new life and as a place to come to terms with personal trauma. However, it should be noted that seminaries are very cautious about admitting people who are in the midst of personal chaos and may not be able to get on with the job of acquiring a theological education. Seminary officials will often suggest a waiting period for applicants who have just been divorced.

Anyone who is a single head of household and an ordained minister is bound to find spiritual and physical strength tested to its limits. It can be difficult, at best, to juggle creatively home life and church life, and there are no easy answers.

Seminaries will vary a great deal in the percentage of their student population that is above thirty years of age. Some seminaries, such as Bangor Theological Seminary in Maine, specialize in older candidates for the ordained ministry. If you fall into this category, it may be worth checking to see how much experience a given seminary has in the training of older students.

While visiting one seminary, I sat down in the dining hall next to a distinguished-looking white-haired gentleman. The wisdom carved in his face led me to believe that he was probably a professor. When I asked if this was the case, he gave a warm laugh and said, "No, I'm a first-year student. I retired from my first career as an engineer and I am preparing for the ministry." His almost fifty years of work before entering seminary will serve this man well.

What is important for older candidates to realize is that their former careers and their former experiences will be of great benefit to them in the ordained ministry. The world can be a wonderful classroom, and added maturity and added exposure to the real world will enrich the ministry of a second-career candidate. The sum of who we are as ordained ministers bears a direct resemblance to where we have been in our lives. God has marvelous and mysterious ways of preparing people to serve.

Many older individuals worry about getting back into the academic routine after being out of school so long. From all indications, older students do very well in the classroom, and most of their fears about reentry into the world of academia are unfounded. Hardly ever is anyone admitted who is incapable of doing seminary work. Older individuals preparing to enter seminary may want to consider taking a local college course first, which will prepare them for the return to academic life.

Most older seminary students have gone through an identity crisis at some time. They are often more sure about who they are and can more realistically appraise their personal strengths and weaknesses. Someone who has done well in another area of life and has felt called to the ordained ministry is a better prospect than an older individual who has never been able to accomplish much of anything and decides to give seminary a whirl.

The job situation as it presently stands in most mainline Protestant denominations is a concern to everyone. It may be a special concern to an older candidate. It is vitally important to understand how the placement system works in the candidate's own denomination.

The counselors at the career counseling centers, the denominational people in charge of candidates, and the local pastor are as much there to assist an older candidate as they are a younger one. It is important to be sure about a sense of call before leaving everything behind and entering seminary.

Whether an individual is a keeper of goats, a dresser of sycamore trees, in the fishing business, or in the Internal Revenue Service, it is impossible to know when Jesus might call out to leave those things behind and, in a special way, command us, "Follow me."

7

The Seminary of Your Choice, or
On Being a Theological Tadpole

We had a streetwise teenage mother and her baby live with us for a period of time. She had been on her own since she was fifteen, and she could get along in any big city without money and without help from the welfare authorities. She had to because she was never willing to wait in line long enough to get assistance.

This young woman could walk into a fast-food restaurant and come out with a large bag of food. She simply said, "I already paid you," and she knew which restaurants had a policy of not arguing about the issue. She was smart as a fox and knew how to survive in the toughest of situations.

If I was going to offer some advice about picking a seminary, I would encourage you to pick one that is streetwise. Attempt to find a seminary that not only can offer you the finest in theological scholarship but also can relate the teaching in the classroom to the day-to-day realities of life in the local church.

I think a definition of a theological seminary might be helpful. The great theologian H. Richard Niebuhr defined the theological school as "intellectual center of the Church's life" (p. 107). To carry this concept one step farther, Niebuhr goes on to refer to a seminary as that special place where "faith seeks understanding" (p. 125).

The theological seminary will attempt to offer some foundation for the faith of the individual who feels called to the ordained ministry. It is an academic center where one comes to deal with theoretical aspects of theology as well as the practical aspects of running a church. It is important in choosing a seminary to discover a school that places a great emphasis on solid theological scholarship, as well as on the day-to-day duties of a pastor in a local church.

To my mind, the primary vocation of a seminary is to train women and men to serve as pastors in the local church. This is where the majority of seminary graduates serve after graduation. To put it bluntly, a seminary graduate should not be accidentally capable of functioning as a pastor in a local church.

There has been concern that while seminaries teach people to be good students, they do not necessarily train students to be professional ministers. Very often seminaries will train students more under an academic model than a professional one. "In the practice of ministry," writes Robert Kemper (pp. 29–30), "the greatest brain in the world is doomed to failure if that brain is not encased in a person with relational skills. As practitioners, we rise and fall not by our individual excellence, but by our interpersonal ministries within a community of faith."

In research done by the Alban Institute entitled *Crossing the Boundary: Between Seminary and Parish,* Roy M. Oswald offers this major concern about education at seminary: "Seminary education can be enhanced if the role and requirements of the profession are clear, just as the knowledge of what a successful tennis player looks like and needs to be able to do can facilitate the development of his skills on the courts" (p. 1). Again, it is vitally important for someone considering a seminary to see that the prospective school has a good balance between the academic and the practical functions of ministry.

Theological seminaries have a difficult job in training students for the ordained ministry, because there is so much to cover in three years and also because it is difficult to predict where and under what circumstances an individual will serve in the future. A pastor going to serve in a Navaho village is going to have concerns different from those of a minister who will be serving in a downtown Detroit church. A great responsibility lies on the individual in seminary to make the education relevant by always being in the process of relating the classroom work with how it may apply to a local church.

Although some of the more theoretical aspects of the seminary curriculum may not seem to be important to a local pastor, they can often be vital as a foundation. Even though few people run up to a pastor and ask her or him to conjugate a Greek verb, it is nonetheless important for a pastor to understand the language and thought forms that color the New Testament. Similarly, systematic theology may not be considered a practical discipline, but when a pastor stands outside an emergency operating room with parents whose child is undergoing surgery, that pastor had better have some theological and pastoral competence.

Achieving the Master of Divinity degree is only the first step toward becoming an ordained minister. There is still a whole lifelong learning process which must occur. Roy Oswald offers this bit of advice to seminary students who are ready to enter full-time service (p. 20): "If you truly believe that you haven't even begun to learn approximately 80% of what you need to know to be an effective pastor, you will begin parish ministry with a disposition that will get you through the first five years of ministry. If, on the other hand, you think you've about got it all together, and simply need to touch it up here and there with some first hand experience, you are on the way to a major depression one to three years down the pike." As the whole church attempts to be sensitive to God's leading, there may be the continuing need to adjust seminary curriculums in order to guarantee that the local church is supplied with high-quality trained professionals.

Finding Your Seminary

If you have gone as far as to consider seminaries, you apparently have more than a passing interest in the vocation of ordained ministry. Seminaries are located in almost every major metropolitan area in the country. Your pastor and denominational executives will be of great assistance to you in locating seminaries that are operated by your denomination, and they will also be able to point out other reputable centers of theological education that may not be sponsored by your particular branch of the Christian church. In addition, I would recommend that you write for a copy of the theological education issues of the *Christian Century* and

Christianity Today. A large number of seminaries advertise in these particular issues.

Once you have received the addresses of seminaries, write to the admissions offices and ask for information. They will gladly send you the catalog and other items related to the school. They may also invite you to campus, either on a prospective students' weekend or at another time that may be more convenient for you. It is important that you give serious consideration to various schools.

It is difficult to generalize about what level of academic standard a seminary may accept. Although your academic standing is certainly an important criterion, most seminaries realize the equal importance of a well-rounded, person-oriented individual. It is fairly safe to say that a B plus average or better in undergraduate work, along with a healthy personality, will gain you entrance into most theological institutions.

The location of most seminaries, in or near major cities, often provides an interesting study in contrasts, because a substantial number of first pastorates will be in small towns or rural areas. Geography often plays an important part in choosing a theological school. You may want to consider a school reasonably close to home, or you may need to find a school in an area where your mate or future mate will be able to locate a job. The climate of a given area or certain cultural advantages may be taken into consideration. Although three years may not seem like a long time, it is important to find a setting that will foster personal and professional growth.

It is imperative to go to a seminary accredited by the Association of Theological Schools and by other appropriate accrediting agencies. You will need to determine the quality of the faculty and their academic standards, because it is vital to find a seminary that will challenge your mind and heart. Often a school's scholarship is shown by the extensiveness of its library.

Living arrangements are an important matter, and you will need to consider the housing arrangements offered by each school you investigate.

I would only consider seminaries that place a high value on fieldwork. Even if you are trained by the best theological minds in the country, if you have no experience in a local church, you will not be ready to function in the pastorate. Be sure to pick a seminary that will train you in the pure and applied science of theology. For an indication of how successful a seminary is at this responsibility, check to see how many of its graduates have been placed.

I would also want a seminary that has something to offer the other members of my family. As has already been discussed, the spouse and other members of an ordained minister's family have to bear heavy strains and stresses. It is important to find a school that will help other family members learn how to cope and relate to the life in the local church.

Although the idea is a bit nebulous, it is important to find a school that will help you to grow and develop within your faith as a Christian, within yourself as a person, and within your calling to the ordained ministry. A good seminary will be deeply concerned about you as a person and will help to enhance your personal characteristics, so that you will realize as much of your God-given potential as possible. As you visit seminaries and speak with members of the faculty, staff, and student body, keep these criteria in the back of your mind.

As a general guideline, I would suggest that you write for at least five catalogs and that you take the initiative to visit at least three seminary campuses. It is difficult to compare the unknown. You will only be able to evaluate one school over another through personal encounters with several schools.

There will probably be several friends who encourage you to attend their seminary. Although a recommendation from someone close can be helpful, I certainly would not choose a school simply because someone you know went there.

Each seminary is unique. Through your investigation and visits you will begin to discover the strengths and weaknesses of each school. It would even be appropriate to be direct by asking the seminary officials, "What is the one thing this seminary has to offer that no other theological school has?" Or "What is the one area of the seminary that needs improvement?" If, at this point, you hope to specialize in one part of the church's work, such as counseling or teaching, it will be important to find a seminary that is strong in the particular area of your interest. A seminary cannot be outstanding in every area.

Be sure to consider a denominational seminary. Your denomination created its seminaries for a specific purpose, and that purpose may have something to do with you. Among other reasons, denominational seminaries will allow you to get the particular courses required by your denomination and also will help you to get a foothold into the life of your particular branch of the Christian church.

There may be some very good reasons for choosing a non-denominational school or a school of another denomination. One large word of caution is in order. If you are rejecting denominational seminaries on the basis that they do not fit into your theological mold, you had better do some deep soul-searching about your relationship to your denomination.

Always be engaged in prayer, and involve God in your decision to enter a particular seminary.

Being a Theological Tadpole

Entering seminary as a new student is a special and exciting experience for many reasons. As a theological tadpole, you will find that any seminary worth its salt will push you to the borders of your faith and to the limits of your world. Then it will take what you believe and help you turn it inside out and upside down and put it all back together again, stronger and more vital than before.

There are some remarkable students who go through seminary totally untouched by the experience. They are there marking time and will leave with exactly what they brought with them. The president of Pittsburgh Theological Seminary, C. Samuel Calian, put it this way (p. 41): "How to go through seminary without learning is almost the hidden wish of some students, who are actually afraid that the seminary process (a necessary means to obtain one's union card) will undermine their 'faith.' Not infrequently a seminarian will share with me the fact that a pastoral friend, a grandfather, or a saintly mother offered the parting advice, 'Now, don't let the seminary take away your faith!' "

Seminary, I have said, is the place where "faith seeks understanding." If a student does not come to seminary with the express purpose of evaluating her or his relationship to God and to humanity, it would be better to stay at home. Seminary is a place for those who are willing to wrestle with the meaning of God in their lives and how they are to respond to their neighbor. As it is in good ministry, so also it is true in superior theological education: there is suffering and a high price to pay for coming to terms with where God is leading us. God called Elijah out of the cave and away from his smallness of mind and heart. Elijah was called to stand upon the mount of the Lord. Only those who can stand in the wide-open spaces and dare to listen to God speaking in a still small voice in all dimensions of life ought to become seminary students.

Theological education is an experience in which an individual must invest both heart and mind. Theology deals with the very source and essence of our being; it deals with ultimate questions that everyone faces; it tackles the problem of suffering; it involves a person in the fact that Jesus Christ died for us. As H. Richard Niebuhr said, "If students are not personally involved in the study of theology they are not yet studying theology at all" (p. 118). It is a special privilege to study at a seminary, where God's concerns, our neighbor's concerns, and our concerns are wrestled with, taught, and lived out.

There are opportunities for personal spiritual growth, but sometimes the devotional life of students is one of the more neglected parts of the seminary experience, as everyone is busy attempting to get on with the job of a theological education. However, in the architectural design of most seminaries it is no mistake that the chapel is the focal point. It is the location where faculty, students, and staff come together in order to worship and to pray. Without this foundational part of a seminary life, all other aspects lose their significance. To quote H. Richard Niebuhr again (p. 131):

> Hence while a community which centers in worship is not a theological school, a theological school in which worship is not a part of the daily and weekly rhythm of activity cannot remain a center of intellectual activity directed toward God. Preaching and

hearing the proclamation is not theological study; but if students of theology, in all their degrees of immaturity and maturity, do not attend to the Word addressed to them as selves their study represents flight from God and self.

It is important, in considering which seminary to choose, to find a theological school that will give growth to the intellect, offer supervised experience in the life of the local church, and give wings to your spiritual existence.

8

Field Education, or
Where the Action Is

A new seminary student had been enrolled for two weeks and still had not seen any action. He kept bugging a professor of pastoral psychology to give him an exciting assignment. The professor finally agreed to allow him to cover at the local general hospital as the student chaplain for one Saturday night. This was the city hospital where you would normally get, on an average, quiet, Saturday evening, the remainders of bar brawls, the overdoses, and anything else you could imagine.

Not long after this new student chaplain went on duty, he was to receive his first case. A man was brought in and quickly pronounced dead. The head nurse brought the man's widow over to the young chaplain. Suddenly this woman grabbed the lapels of the unsuspecting seminary student and began jerking him up and down off the floor, while screaming into his face, "Do something, do something, do something!" Flustered, he began screaming back at her, "What do you want me to do? What do you want me to do?" All of a sudden she stopped bouncing him up and down and, in the middle of her hysteria, quietly asked him, "You're new at this, aren't you?" He responded, "Yes, ma'am! I sure am, and we are going to learn our way together through this!"

Supervised ministry, field education, the practice of ministry, or whatever name a seminary gives to on-the-job training is an invaluable part of seminary education. This is where you learn, under supervision and with reflection, to do ministry by doing it.

Different seminaries conduct field education in different ways. Most seminaries generally require a certain amount of participation in supervised ministry to graduate, and I would not even consider a seminary that did not place a high value on this type of experience. Many seminary students participate in a field education experience their first semester and continue until the day of graduation.

Students will be interviewed, as a general rule, for several field education positions and eventually, through a matching process, will secure a position. During the school year, a student works on the job evenings and/or weekends and under the supervision of an ordained minister.

Except for certain types of positions, these are paying jobs, and this is often a basic source of income for the seminary student. The real value, however, can only be measured by the experience gained in being an apprentice. This is where you can begin to relate your classroom work to practical experience. It may be the first time you preach or the first time you lead a youth group. It may be the first time you are with a dying patient or the first time you work with the disadvantaged.

Your supervising minister is required to meet with you on a regular basis in order to discuss with you what you have been doing. This person often becomes a real friend you can trust, as he or she evaluates your performance in the practice of ministry.

Field education can be pretty well summarized by three categories: church positions, clinical training, and community organizations. If your first experience is in a church position, you will often be called a seminary assistant. Your job description will be known during the interviewing process, and you will probably get varied experience working in the church: a little preaching, leading in worship, teaching, visiting, and counseling. Chances are you will be doing a lot of what strikes terror in the hearts of many—youth work. Since many seminarians are reasonably young, churches assume that they will relate well to young people, which is not necessarily a logical conclusion. Unfortunately, a major weakness in a lot of seminary curricula is a lack of courses on youth ministry. If you do become involved in youth work, I hope you will not pass it off as a second-class ministry; good professional youth ministers are few and far between.

There are generally a few positions open for student pastors. These are normally assignments reserved for seniors, where a student has a small congregation that is unable to afford a full-time professional minister. Some seminaries require that a student take a reduced class load, in order to compensate for the extra time it takes to serve such a pastorate.

One of my suggestions is that seminary students try to get experience in several positions. Sometimes students will become very comfortable in one situation and will stay put, instead of interviewing for a new position. There are advantages to continuing in a position over a period of time, but exposure will be limited. The variety and richness of experience, at this stage in the game, should far outweigh any advantages of long-term work.

Supervised ministry also occurs in clinical settings: a hospital, a prison, a mental health facility, a juvenile detention center, a home for the physically disabled. A program known as Clinical Pastoral Education is often involved with these settings. C.P.E. is supervised training combined with practical experience in a clinical setting, under a chaplain who has advanced training in pastoral psychology. As part of this excellent training process, students meet with the chaplain on a regular basis for interpersonal growth. The dynamics of what is happening within you are combined with how effectively you are relating to the functions of a chaplain.

One of the techniques used within C.P.E. group meetings is the periodic writing of "verbatims." A verbatim is writing out a conversation, both sides of it, that a student chaplain has with a patient. This conversation is then scrutinized by the other students and the supervisor. What was said, why it was said, the patient's response to the conversation, the effect of the conversation, how it could have been more effective, what the patient was really trying to get at, and the student chaplain's feelings toward the patient are closely examined. It is a process whereby students learn as much about themselves as they do about the practice of ministry.

It is my feeling that at least one unit of Clinical Pastoral Education should be a requirement to graduate from seminary. It is far too valuable an experience to pass up. This may be the best opportunity for seminary students to relate and correlate themselves with their roles as professional ministers. It is exactly in this area that so much of the pain of the ordained ministry is felt. This clinical experience may be just what the doctor ordered for coping with the stresses and strains associated with most professional ministries.

The third setting where fieldwork is conducted is in the community. This may mean working in a local recreation program, a neighborhood ministry, a children's home, or a community service agency. This experience is especially valuable to someone who will be working later in an inner-city ministry or any other type that makes use of community services on a regular basis. Although this work can prove to be valuable because it involves agencies who are attempting to meet human need, it ought to be balanced with church and clinical training.

There are often very specific fieldwork positions open to a limited number of seminary students. They may be related to prophetic areas, such as civil rights, or they may deal with a special job with the seminary faculty or staff. These vary a great deal from school to school and from one year to the next.

Most seminaries pretty well close down during the summer months, except for intensive language courses. This is a great time to gain field education experience on a full-time basis for the three summer months. There is normally a wide variety of openings available for summer fieldwork, near the seminary or at locations across the country. Among other types of opportunities, a Christian ministry in the National Parks hires a large number of seminary students to lead worship services, with the student being given a secular park-related job.

The three years of seminary are divided into the junior year, the middler year, and the senior year. Many students opt to take a year off in between their middler year and their senior year. At a number of seminaries, this appears to be the norm rather than the exception. The choice of positions is generally large for someone who decides to have an intern year, because there are more opportunities than there are students to fill them.

The advantages of an intern year are many. One would be just taking a break from the rigors of the classroom. It may be necessary to shore up finances. And experience at this point in one's education can help to focus on really understanding the practical aspects and nature of ministry. Many seminarians come back from an intern year with a better understanding of what they wish to get out of the classroom, and they are often more deeply committed to finishing their final year.

International experiences are also a possibility, as an intern year or as a chance to study abroad. If this looks attractive to you, it is important to consider the options and begin working out the details early in your seminary career. Being a seminary intern in a mission in Zaire or studying for a year in Edinburgh can offer a global dimension to your education and spiritual life.

The disadvantages of an intern year are probably obvious: it delays the whole process for a year. Each individual will need to determine how the scales balance on this issue. It is an option and opportunity for every seminary student that ought to be given serious consideration.

The importance and value of field education plus quality supervision cannot be overstated. It is as important to a seminary student preparing to be a pastor as is academic training in Bible or theology. The value of supervised ministry has often been understated in the total seminary experience. As H. Richard Niebuhr suggests (p. 128):

> One cannot understand the meaning of preaching in the total work of the Church apart from direct personal hearing and proclamation of the gospel, nor know the character of worship, its direction, the requirements it makes on the self and its relations to proclamation and service unless one is a worshiper. How shall one understand Christian education in theory without engaging in it as teacher and student, or church administration without participation in the organized common life of a Christian community?

Field education is that part of the seminary experience in which one learns to do ministry by doing it under supervision and with a good amount of reflection. What most seminary students come quickly to realize is that authentic ministry does not wait for ordination. Field education is not like playing at ministry, it is ministry.

H. Richard Niebuhr comments that "all too often 'field work' is regarded and directed as though its purpose were the acquisition of skills for future use" (p. 131). However, as Niebuhr points out, field education brings ministry right up and into the present moment. Field education is much more than an activity in which a student prepares for that someday when he or she will be capable of doing ministry. People cannot be viewed as guinea pigs on whom a student practices ministering.

Without the theological training of the classroom, field education would be a shallow way to prepare for the ordained ministry. But the reverse is also true. Without practical training, theoretical training in a seminary classroom alone would be like trying to teach a person to ride a bicycle by reading a book. The pure science and the applied science of theology need to be held in proper tension and dialogue.

9

Financing a Seminary Education, or
Mary, Welcome to the Ark

Bob and Mary fell in love and planned to get married following Bob's first year at seminary. Finances are a concern for every young couple, especially if one of them is a full-time student, so Bob was elated when the church he was working in as a seminary assistant generously offered him a house to live in, next to the church, for free. He promptly named it the Ark; mud left by an Ohio River flood twenty-five years earlier was still caked on the ceilings.

Bob was a hardy soul, who could often be found eating Hamburger Helper for several days in a row, which is not really so bad until you consider that Bob didn't add hamburger to it. One weekend, Mary, his betrothed, came to visit, and we all went along while Bob showed Mary their first nest.

Mary, somewhat to our surprise, seemed to be reasonably happy with the Ark as Bob proudly pointed out all its benefits. (I do not remember his mentioning that the house had been condemned by the city and that next year, when an urban development project was started, it would be torn down.) I am sure Mary would have been delighted to live in a tepee in the middle of Death Valley, as long as she was with Bob. Actually, all was going very well until Mary excused herself to use the bathroom. Soon after she closed the door, a sudden noise and then a scream was heard. Mary had fallen through the floor.

Although most seminary students do not take vows of poverty, sometimes it may feel like that. And, as you remember from Dr.

Barrow's research discussed in chapter 4, the number-one concern among married students at Columbia Theological Seminary was financial strain.

Now it is not really practical to attempt to be very specific about the cost of a seminary education, but a little general conversation about this area may be important.

Substantial amounts of financial aid are given to students who need it. However, as a result of certain regulations, it may be impossible to know exactly how much aid you may be eligible to receive from a seminary until you are actually enrolled. The general procedure moves along these lines. You (and your spouse, if you are married) sit down with the financial aid director. Together you list all your sources of income in one column and all your anticipated expenses in a parallel column. The difference between your anticipated income and your anticipated expenses is your "gap." The financial aid director will help you to fill this gap in several ways.

You will need to consider ways in which you can generate income. Savings are one possibility. If, though, you are a person just graduating from college, the chances of your having a large amount of extra cash lying around are pretty slim. However, if you are older and have a substantial amount in savings, the financial aid office takes this into consideration and may expect you to use a portion of your savings.

Your home church is often a very basic supporter of your calling to the professional ministry. Often local churches are delighted to aid you financially, and financial aid officers are always glad to drop a note to your church to express how meaningful this would be.

The local judicatory, conference, or presbytery may have some monies set aside or some scholarships for people just like you. Again, seminary financial aid officers are very proficient at helping you discover sources of support. They will want to be sure all other sources of support for you have been located before they decide what the seminary can contribute to your education.

A working spouse can often be the largest contributor to the financial well-being of the family. The seminary is often asked to recommend students' spouses to employers in the community, so they may even be able to help with job leads.

Parents may be another source of support. They obviously have an investment in your life. This source, however, needs to be carefully balanced. If they have just put you through college, your parents may have exhausted their resources on your undergraduate work. Also, there comes a time in life when it is important for you to be fully independent. And if you are older, you would probably not expect much more financial support from your parents. Do not automatically reject this possible source, but be sure to weigh it carefully. Whenever anyone wishes to contribute to your education, there are generally ways it can be done to provide a tax advantage. Check with the financial aid officer.

Working is a way of continuing to allow yourself the privilege of eating. Many seminaries require field education work, as we saw in the previous chapter. Generally these positions pay a stipend or contribute toward a scholarship for you. Although you will not become rich with one of these positions, it is valuable not only from a monetary consideration but also from the standpoint of experience.

In addition to fieldwork, every seminary hires students to do kitchen work, yard work, maintenance work, library work, and an assortment of other jobs. Employment outside the seminary is also a possibility. However, your main aim is to gain a good seminary experience, which can be destroyed by becoming over-committed both to work and to school. Be careful about maintaining a good balance between school, work, and personal time.

Various agencies and institutions with philanthropic funds are often willing to provide assistance to seminary students. It will certainly be worth your while to check into all possible sources for surviving the seminary years.

Student loans of various kinds are available to you, with the stipulation that there will be no interest until graduation. Loans can be helpful, but be careful about incurring a large debt. You are not a medical student with the promise of taking home a large salary at a not-too-distant time. Seminary officials will also be concerned that you not go too deeply into debt.

After all other sources have been exhausted, the seminary will often chip in, often in a big way. Most seminaries give the majority of their students some sort of financial assistance, probably averaging in the neighborhood of $1,000 plus per year. This varies a great deal, however. The seminary itself generates its monetary support from various sources and what it will be able to offer is directly connected to its revenue.

Seminary financial officials and seminary students want to be fair about giving and receiving financial aid. I have never known anyone who left seminary as a result of a dire financial predicament. I am sure some students have indeed left for financial reasons, but, all else being equal, most seminaries will not allow a student to leave because of a mere lack of cash. You can trust the financial aid office to help you as best and as fairly as is possible. Whereas there are generally small amounts of financial aid at the college level, there are large amounts programmed into a seminary's master budget for the Master of Divinity students.

If you know seminary is in your future, it would be advisable to contact the financial aid offices at the various seminaries that you are considering. Every seminary has certain types of scholarships for which you may be eligible. One seminary has a Greek or Latin scholarship given to incoming students who have had Greek or Latin in college. This scholarship is part of a will and cannot be changed. With fewer and fewer colleges offering Greek and Latin, the school is having a hard time giving away this money. If your denomination requires Greek, it is as easy to take it on the college level as it is in seminary. Search carefully for scholarships at the seminaries you may be interested in attending. You may be surprised!

I think we can qualify this issue a little further according to the denomination of the seminary, if any. According to Christopher Walters-Bugbee (pp. 98–99), the average tuition at seminaries increased from $559 in 1970 to only $1,223 in 1978, which was a mere 118 percent increase over an eight-year period. These figures are even a little low, because the Southern Baptist and Lutheran seminaries have rather low tuitions, thanks to their being generously supported by their denominations. At the other end of the scale, where a seminary, such as Yale, has no denominational identity, the tuition is extremely high.

Like all phases of the life of the church, these inflationary times put a great financial strain on providing good theological education. The cost is bound to affect the average seminary student, who is attempting to live on a modest level.

There may even be some creative ways in which you can help yourself through seminary. For example, house-sitting is a possibility in most communities. There are individuals who would be anxious to have a seminary student take care of their place. Who knows, you may even live in an Ark.

Good budgeting is probably going to be a very important part of guaranteeing a good seminary experience. Charlie Shedd considers his financial condition with his daughter, Karen (pp. 118–119), as he takes a nostalgic journey back to his seminary days:

My dear Karen,

In our married days at the seminary we went often to the warehouses on grocer's row. There was one place where they stacked cans of food clear up to the ceiling. It was like standing before a mountain of tin. There were big cans, little cans, tall cans, short cans, round, square, oblong, flat—cans of every size, shape, and condition.

There was, however, this one difference between the cans here and those you see on your grocer's shelves. These had no labels. Because of this slight omission they were for sale at three cents per can. The sorters had tossed them aside as "damaged," which meant anything from a major dent to some minor flaw which could only be noted by the inspector's eye

The man who ran the warehouse guaranteed this one thing—there was food of some variety in each can. He also claimed that nothing was spoiled, but, as he said, "for three cents what you gonna lose? You pay your money and take your choice."

Do you know how to tell the difference between peaches and plums by the shake of the can? Could you, by ear, distinguish carrots from corn? Well, your mother and I became well-nigh infallible as shakers of edibles.

Of course, no one is perfect; so, we sometimes drew chili for dessert. It sounds like fruit cocktail! Thank goodness, we had an icebox and plastic covers were cheap; so, we lived it up and laughed and ate away. In fact, it was great fun and we looked forward to our semi-monthly outing to the can hills.

For three dollars on payday we could purchase one hundred cans of nourishment, and the man was right—it was all palatable and all good! Sure, there were times when we wished we might be free of this small-change living and shop at the stores with the nice folks. But as we look back on it now, we list those days with our happiest memories.

Everybody's financial situation is different, and every seminary student receives income from various sources. For most, there is about a break-even dimension between income and expenses. How this is achieved sometimes only God knows. If you live on a seminary campus, you will know that everyone else's financial plight will be just about as bad as yours.

Although the most interesting information about a seminary will not be listed in the catalog on the pages that describe the cost, the scholarships, and the financial aid, this is an area to explore fully.

The call to the professional ministry can be a painful task, requiring a great amount of personal sacrifice. This sacrifice, probably more for some than others, may be revealed in dollars and cents. How an individual handles this financial aspect may say a lot about that person's spirit, maybe about a spouse's commitment, and even maybe how well suited one is for the vocation of a professional minister.

10

Women and the Ordained Ministry, or Discrimination Is Alive and Well in the Church

Dorothy Fowler has recalled this experience (see Schaller, ed., pp. 26–27), which took place when she was serving as the pastor of the United Methodist Church in Wink, Texas.

> Toward the end of my fourth year as pastor at Wink, the chairperson of the administrative board brought me a full-length mirror to install in my study. My mother watched me while I adjusted my robe and stole in front of it, and she said to the board chairperson, "You know, one of these days you'll have a male minister here, and with that flattering mirror you will never get him out of here to preach."
>
> "Oh, no," the board chairperson assured her, "we don't want any male preachers here."
>
> I smiled to myself as I recalled the words of the Episcopal priest who had shared a wedding with me in our church shortly after my appointment.
>
> "Congregations will never accept women pastors," he had said. "Never."
>
> "Perhaps not," I had replied. "But never is a long, long time."

Over the past fifteen years, the most dramatic occurrence within most Protestant seminaries has been the large number of women preparing for the ordained ministry. According to annual reports summarized in the *Yearbook of American and Canadian Churches,* in 1972—when sex distribution information was first requested—there were only 3,358 women enrolled in the member seminaries of the Association of Theological Schools, comprising 10.2 percent of the total. Each year this total has steadily risen, and in 1983 there were 13,451 women enrolled, or 24.4 percent of the total. This increase in the number of women is even more striking when you realize that, of the 195 seminaries belonging to the A.T.S., many are Roman Catholic or other denominations that do not recognize the ordination of women. From all indications, the day is rapidly approaching when the student bodies of mainline Protestant seminaries will be made up of equal numbers of men and women.

Primarily through the advent of the women's movement, women are now entering the once male-dominated church leadership structure. Whether or not women should be ordained has been a burning issue over the last ten to fifteen years. The ordination of women is not only a question for women, it is also of concern to men, and particularly men in leadership positions in the church.

Taking the historical view, we know that the biblical narrative grew out of a patriarchal society, where women had few rights. The Bible was not written in a cultural vacuum. It is important to separate the message of the Bible from the culture of biblical times.

If we are completely honest in our examination, we must admit that women were not always highly regarded. Women in the Bible primarily gained their status from being wives and mothers; they gained their worth through their husbands and children, particularly male children. In Old Testament times there was not much of a developed sense of the afterlife, and it was believed that individuals lived on through their children. It was extremely important to have sons to carry on the name. Throughout the biblical narrative it is possible to see cultural conditioning producing an obvious double standard.

In exploring the role of women in biblical culture (which may not be all that different from what many people assume to be the proper role of women in today's world), we find some radical and revolutionary passages, which confront us with a new reality. The apostle Paul, who is often accused of being chauvinistic, is the one who wrote: "There is neither Jew nor Greek, there is neither slave nor free, there is neither male nor female; for you are all one in Christ Jesus" (Galatians 3:28). Paul is telling us that in the act of baptism, in the new life we receive in Christ, all earthly distinctions are torn down. There is no difference between male and female.

Jesus had an interesting encounter with Martha and Mary when he went to their home. While Martha was busy preparing a meal in the kitchen, Mary was sitting with Jesus and learning from his teachings. Martha got angry and came out of the kitchen to demand that Jesus tell Mary to get her lazy bones into the kitchen and do some work. Jesus, once again, did the unexpected thing. He told Martha that she was too busy preparing a meal and that Mary was gaining more from his visit because she was learning from his teachings.

If we remember that the main call, the foundational call, is the call to "be a Christian," then when we are discussing the ordination of women, we are really engaged in a dialogue about a secondary call. A secondary call does not mean an unimportant call, but it does mean that it is less significant than the paramount call to every Christian. It seems inconsistent that women are encouraged to accept the call to be a Christian and then discouraged from accepting a secondary call to the ordained ministry.

Feelings can run high about this issue, and it is important for every Christian, and particularly the women and men preparing for the ordained ministry to work through this concern from a historical, theological, and biblical perspective. Within many denominations that ordain women, the most striking assurance that God calls women to ordained ministry is the sheer numbers of women enrolled in Master of Divinity programs, as well as those women who are already ordained.

Pioneers

The first major wave of female seminary students to move into seminary and then into positions of leadership within the local church occurred during the early and middle 1970s. These women were considered the pioneers, the first major group of women to really rock the ecclesiastical boat. During this time, women seminary students were often seen, fairly or unfairly, as being a bit radical, revolutionary, and angry.

It appears as if there is now a new era for women in seminary and entering into the leadership of the church. There seems to be less anger and a more varied stance along the theological spectrum. Dr. Frank Williams, former Director of the Mid-West

Career Development Center, has said, "On the average, women candidates are slightly superior to the male counterparts that we are seeing, regarding emotional well-being, intentionality, and possession of capabilities enhancing potential ministry. They are also less angry."

A Woman's Call

In consideration of a call to the ordained ministry, it is not possible to say that a woman's call is different from a man's. However, one difficulty many women face is that often they will not have any role models. Many female seminary students in interviews have said that they had not even met a woman ordained minister before entering seminary.

With the lack of role models, women will sometimes feel a less developed sense of the call to ministry. This does not mean that their call is weaker. It apparently stems from the fact that they have not seen a woman fulfill the role. A number of women students whom I interviewed suggest that after one semester at seminary a strong sense of call forms for many women. Many female seminarians feel that their call is strong—and has to be strong—because of the extra hurdles women have to face within the life of the church.

The majority of men headed for seminary are reinforced in their decision by the members of their families, their friends, and their pastors. Although there are some definite exceptions, males are often openly encouraged in their sense of calling and in their decision to enter seminary. The same is not always true for women. "Diane Pierce, a bespectacled, determined young Congregational minister from Connecticut, said she had to steel herself on the night of her ordination because her mother broke down and cried, 'It's all my fault'" (quoted by the Proctors, p. 27). And one mother, whose daughter was in seminary, implied to her bridge club that her daughter was doing graduate work in a totally unrelated area.

Although women are becoming more accepted in the role of pastors, it is not unusual for a woman candidate to get a mixed reaction to her intention to study for the ordained ministry. Many women are actually discouraged, by family members, by friends, and even by their local pastors. The discouragement is generally not because of potential or gifts, but because of the sheer biological fact of being female.

What becomes very important for a woman is the careful discernment of gifts. There are men who are discouraged from entering the ordained ministry for a variety of reasons. Pastors, parents, candidates' committees, church counselors, and others may discourage a man for good reasons. There may also be legitimate reasons for not encouraging a woman to pursue the ordained ministry, reasons which have nothing to do with her sex. A potential female candidate will need to be careful to sort through whatever discouragement may come her way. She will need to sift through the feedback from others and objectively decide whether the reservations are merely due to her sex or whether they are legitimate. Attempting to discover her adviser's view on women in the ordained ministry in general will be a helpful way of offering a better focus.

A woman struggling with a possible call to the ordained ministry will be helped by talking to a female pastor. Only another woman who has moved through similar experiences of being encouraged and discouraged can really know what it is like. It is important for a woman candidate to see and know how at least one other woman functions in the role of pastor. Those who are responsible for candidates should have at least one woman pastor among them.

Women who are discouraged from pursuing a call on the basis of their sex have an extra burden right from the beginning. It is especially difficult to be discouraged by people you love. There is always a hope that others might be able to grow into a more accepting stance, but this is not always possible. Sometimes it is necessary to accept other people's limitations.

Seminary

The actual decision to enter seminary may not be any more difficult for a woman than for a man. The only difference might come in the number of extra factors women have to take into consideration. The main factor is still the role identification problem. It is a tougher decision to follow a call if family members, friends, and the local pastor are not supportive.

Women, like men, may have family considerations of a spouse and children. The decision to move to a seminary campus and leave familiar people and places behind can be traumatic. There is also a large financial consideration which must be worked out in order to meet expected needs. Although it should not be any more difficult for a husband and children to pull up roots than it would be for a wife and children to move, in reality it appears to be more complicated. Although we are working toward equal rights, there is still a long way to go.

An increasing number of women are attending seminary on a part-time basis. This is especially true of seminaries located in metropolitan areas, where commuting to a local seminary becomes an option. This option appears to be especially attractive to a woman who is married and has children. In this way, these women are able to pursue ordination education over a period of several years, while continuing to be engaged in other areas of life they find equally meaningful or necessary.

On the whole, most women appear to find seminary life to be supportive. There always appear to be male students who are unsure about women becoming ordained ministers, but generally they are few. Most women find the seminary community to be a setting that will affirm their gifts and potential as they pursue their goal of ordination.

One part of the seminary experience that is not as ideal as it should be for women is the field education process. When it comes to securing a position in a church in order to gain practical experience, the options are often more limited for women students. Very early, women students are confronted with the fact that church people on the local level are not necessarily going to welcome them with open arms.

One woman applied for a field education position at a local church and was indeed hired. However, the warning was clear when the chairperson of the committee said to her, "You are the first woman minister we have had in our church. If you are a flop, it will be a disaster." The female seminarian's sense of humor came into play and she responded, "Well, you are the first church I have ever worked for. If you are a flop, I will never work for another church."

Placement

Women have traditionally played and been seen in supportive, caring, and helping roles. Women are often viewed as more approachable when it comes to problems. A large part of a pastor's job is nurturing people in various ways. Thus, women, who seem culturally conditioned to be more sensitive than men, are really well suited for the profession.

The Rev. Abigail Evans, during an interview, was asked about whether or not her sex would be a hindrance to her ministry. "No, I think it would be an asset. . . . First of all, the majority of church members are women. Secondly, I think there's an innate feminine ability to care and be concerned and open to people—an ability that isn't necessarily true of a man." (Quoted by the Proctors, p. 30.)

On the other side of the ledger, women "traditionally" are not seen in roles of power and authority. This may explain why some congregations are less willing to listen to a female preacher. Maybe this is also the reason women may be viewed as possibly being less effective when it comes to managing church finances or being a trustee of a church building. And so as not to be too hard on males at this point, let it be noted that it is often the female members of a congregation who are most opposed to women in the pulpit.

Even though women obviously have real gifts to offer the church as ordained ministers, they are not readily accepted into positions of leadership. At least four years of college and three years of graduate study is a long time to prepare for any vocation, not to mention the enormous financial investment. And even when the church of Jesus Christ is called to be living on the boundaries of new life, we find that discrimination is alive and well in the church.

A report of the Presbyterian Panel of April 1980 concerning the placement of women as United Presbyterian Church clergy concluded that most of the panelists surveyed felt that a woman being recommended by a Pastoral Nominating Committee would create problems and division within the congregation. C. Samuel Calian is accurate when he states, "The female pastor for the immediate future will be frustrated as she discovers time after time that the church at the grass roots level is not an equal opportunity employer" (p. 51).

The real problem regarding placement for women is not the first call out of seminary. Although many churches will not consider a female pastor, most women will eventually get placed if they are open to moving. It is fair to say, though, that the opportunities for female graduates are definitely less numerous than they are for their male counterparts.

After the first call, it is difficult for women to move on to a larger parish or to become the head of staff in a church. Although this holds true to a degree for men, it is much more difficult for women seeking advancement in the church structure on the local level.

The Future

It is amazing what an impact women have made on the life of the church in recent years, both as theologians and as pastors. Considering the large number of women continuing to prepare for the ordained ministry, the church increasingly will see women occupying positions of leadership in the local and national church. I believe the day will come when the leadership of the church will be roughly made up of the sex ratio within churches. The seeds have been planted and the dynamics are in motion, but, like any major revolution, it is often a slow, difficult, and frustrating process.

It is an exciting time for women in many areas of endeavor, including the church. We need the equal leadership of women within the church, and we need women who are willing to struggle to make this happen. As in the ministry in general, the call to serve God is never an easy one. Over and over again we discover that authentic ministry emerges from our human predicament, which is very closely related to our sex.

Maribeth Blackman-Sexton speaks about her experiences in the pastorate (in Schaller, ed., pp. 60–61):

Above all, however, this crazy career I have chosen is exciting. It is exciting to be on the cutting edge of a growing movement. It is exciting to walk into the pulpit on Sunday morning and know that I belong there. It is exciting to be part of a group that seeks to make visible, within the community of the faithful, the feminine half of the divine image. It is exciting when "Mrs. Smith," an elderly member of a more conservative church in the community, can say following a service in which we participated together, "The more I hear you, the more I am convinced that a woman can do anything." Not every person I come into contact with is so easily convinced, but I do see changes taking place in people's attitudes and responsiveness.

Women, just like men, must respond to God's call. It is not a matter of being male or female. It is a matter of faithfulness.

11

Different Types of Ministry, or You Don't Have to Preach to Preach

The young Baptist preacher had just graduated from seminary. When he delivered his first sermon, the people in the back of the sanctuary could not hear him. This went on for several Sundays, until finally a man stood up in the back row, right in the middle of the sermon, and said, "Brother Preacher, we can't hear what you're saying." A man seated in the front row stood up, turned around to the man in the back row, and said to him, "Sit down, brother, and praise the Lord!"

The local pastorate is only one setting in which professional ministers labor. We often refer to non-parish clergy as being engaged in specialized ministry. We have all sorts of names for people who serve in places outside the local parish. The underlying assumption is that true ministry really occurs only in the local pastorate. All other forms of ministry are of a lesser value. Specialized ministries are often regarded as the odd ministries.

A *Joint Report* in 1981 found that among every ten ministers of the Word and Sacrament in the Presbyterian Church (U.S.A.) there are approximately three who are engaged in what frequently are called specialized ministries. This same report says that "at least fifty percent of all ordained ministers will serve in some form of specialized ministry prior to retirement" (p. N-47). If you are headed for the ordained ministry, you very well might be engaged in a specialized ministry at some point or even throughout your career. This is even more true if you happen to be female, since proportionately more women serve in specialized ministry.

The varieties of service include, in addition to the ministry of the local church, military chaplains, hospital chaplains, prison chaplains, church administration, higher education, pastoral counseling, and so on.

A major problem when contemplating non-parish clergy comes in attempting to decide how elastic the call to ordained ministry can be. Is a person serving as a hospital chaplain considered to be engaged in a legitimate ordained ministry? How about an ordained minister who serves in a government counseling agency? Whole denominations are grappling with the issue of what kind of call can be considered as legitimate for ordination.

Traditionally, a call to the ordained ministry is for a person who regularly preaches the Word and administers the Sacraments. The church is fully aware of the fact that a healthy percentage of its ordained ministers are not engaged in such an activity. Thus it becomes theologically and pragmatically difficult to determine what is and what is not a legitimate calling.

If you seek to specialize, you may very well have to justify your ministry to your denomination, if it is of an unusual nature. To my mind, if an individual has received the proper training and denominational backing and is engaged in a ministry in support of the Word and Sacraments, there is little reason to quibble about ordination. Once again, if we consider the call to be a Christian as the paramount call, we do not need to be overly parochial about the form a call to ordained ministry may take. Let us now briefly explore some areas of service other than the local church.

Ordained ministers serve as administrators in the various agencies and governing bodies of the church. Although this may seem to be an unlikely step out of seminary, it may be of interest to you. You may want to prepare intentionally for this goal by gaining a good background in church order and administration.

Mission work is another area of service. We now often refer to individuals in this field as fraternal workers instead of missionaries. The emphasis of most modern mission projects has changed with the name. We are now less paternalistic and more concerned with training local people to help their own people. Mission work is on a more cooperative basis; there are even missionaries from other parts of the globe who come to the United States. And if ever there is a nation on earth that could use a little missionary influence, it would have to be ours.

As I am sure you know, clergy are not the only people needed in the mission field—abroad or at home. There is a need for people with backgrounds in everything from agriculture to medicine to teaching. If mission work appeals to you, get in touch with the national office of your denomination that trains, recruits, and sends fraternal workers; they will have some helpful advice for you. The command of a useful foreign language and some specialized skills are often of great help in carrying out modern fraternal work. Unfortunately, because of budget problems, a lot of denominations are not doing as much in this ministry of the church as they would like.

Pastoral counseling is a big area in which people specialize. With added expertise, some people serve as chaplains in a variety of institutional settings. If you are interested in serving as a chaplain in a hospital, psychiatric institution, prison, or detention facility, you will need to be sure to get some early experience in Clinical Pastoral Education.

There are also pastoral counselors who do counseling as a full-time vocation. This may be in conjunction with a church, a mental health facility, or an agency of the church. There are a number of professional organizations and accrediting bodies that can help you if you plan to specialize in a counseling ministry.

Serving as a college chaplain is another ministry that many consider an attractive possibility. You may want to contact the agency within your denomination in charge of higher education ministry and the United Ministries in Higher Education organization, which helps to coordinate ministry on college and university campuses. A college chaplain often does a great deal of counseling, so some extra work in this area would be advisable. Some college chaplains do a little teaching, so a college may require a chaplain to have an advanced academic degree.

Teaching is another area in which professional ministers specialize, this is normally achieved through an advanced degree. The teaching field is crowded, but colleges and universities need professors of philosophy and religion and other related areas.

Seminaries, of course, also hire professors. If this is your goal, you will want to be careful about the selection of the advanced degree you pursue.

Ordained ministers also serve in social ministries. Social ministry, or prophetic ministry, is being sensitive to the poor, the downtrodden, the outcast, and the "elephant people" of the twentieth century. These ministries might be anything from organizing mountain folk to promoting the needs of the hungry at home or abroad. You might be engaged in creating better living conditions for a slum area of a city or providing some alternative ways of life for prostitutes.

Other ways in which ordained ministers can specialize within the church include serving as church fund raisers, librarians at theological institutions, staff people at church colleges, and administrators of church nursing homes.

The Military Chaplaincy

The military chaplaincy is an unusual ministry for several reasons, and over the past several years there has been much discussion about clergy serving as military officers. The church and state separation is not very separate, when it comes to ordained ministers serving in the Armed Forces. This issue was a very sensitive one during the Vietnam War, when certain organizations were calling for the withdrawal of chaplains during this time in our nation's history.

On behalf of Clergy and Laity Concerned About Vietnam, Harvey Cox (no relation) edited a book entitled *Military Chaplains* that was highly critical of the church's involvement in the military. I am not simply dragging up past history for the sake of controversy, but to point out that professional ministers serving as officers in the Armed Forces assume a somewhat ambiguous position. Wearing uniforms and holding rank make them subject to military regulations. At the same time, ordained ministers are under total obligation to their commitment to Christ, to their ordination vows, and to their denomination. The present tendency of those in this difficulty is to recognize the dichotomy and attempt to live with it. It takes a special person to live creatively within this paradox.

Chaplain Richard Hutcheson has written a marvelous book titled *The Churches and the Chaplaincy*. If you have an interest in serving as a military chaplain, this book is a must! Hutcheson recalls an incident (p. 32) where the church–military tension came into play for him. It seems a commander had a fatherly interest in a young clerk in his office. This young clerk proposed to an Oriental girl of the Buddhist faith. The girl accepted, and the commander called the chaplain.

> He called me to make the necessary arrangements. I advised him that I could only perform Christian weddings, and that I would not be able to officiate at a ceremony involving a Buddhist girl. The commanding officer exploded. "What do you mean you can't marry them? You're in the Navy, aren't you? You'll marry who I tell you to marry." It took some tall talking on my part to convince him that I was not only in the Navy, but also in my church, and that my authority to perform marriages was controlled not by the former but by the latter.

Beyond the problem of loyalty to Christ versus Caesar, the chaplaincy is a ministry performed in an unusual setting and often under unusual circumstances. The local church environment and the models for ministry based on the local church setup are not very compatible for effective ministry within the military establishment. Hutcheson quotes a clergyperson (p. 35) who went from a local church into a military chaplaincy:

> As a civilian minister, I was a person of standing within the community. . . . Then I entered a strange world in which I had to shout, "Attention on deck!" when someone, perhaps no older than me but clearly identified as an authority figure, entered the room. I learned to stand in a rigid brace at morning inspection while someone with more stripes on his sleeve looked me up and down as if I were a horse. I can only describe the experience as "culture shock."

The military chaplaincy is a ministry in which you participate with your parishioners and endure the same set of circumstances they endure. It is a ministry primarily within an institution peopled by blue-collar young adults, where a lot of crises occur. The chaplain as a friend, confidant, confessor, and counselor is very important. Long separations, particularly in the Navy, create special hardships on members of the Armed Forces and their relationships. This specialized ministry does not center around the chapel or worship experience as much as it centers around the marketplace. The chaplain has an opportunity to work on an ecumenical team. The people to whom a chaplain ministers are moved on a regular basis. In addition, the chaplain is constantly in touch with people who have nothing to do with the church.

"The military chaplain," writes Hutcheson, "is probably the only minister in Christendom who habitually sees his parishioners in their skivy drawers" (p. 48). As women chaplains become more prominent and women in the military become more common, this will be altered. But the feeling is correct that military chaplains deal with the raw material of life, where their parishioners really are, as opposed to only seeing people in their Sunday best.

The issues, as well as the opportunities, for a military chaplain are too far-reaching and complicated for a brief statement. If you wish to become a chaplain in the military, learn the procedure set up by your denomination. You will be loaned to the military on behalf of your denomination, and you only remain a chaplain at the grace of your denomination.

You must be:

A citizen of the United States
Under 33 years of age (some exceptions)
Physically qualified
Ordained and endorsed by your denomination
Experienced (active ministry in a local church)
Checked by national agency

The armed services request a proportionate percentage of clergy of a given denomination as represented in the national population. Thus, if there are more Baptists in the United States than Episcopalians, there will be more Baptist clergy serving as military chaplains

There is a chaplain candidate program in which, during a summer of your seminary career, you can attend a chaplain's school with the approval of your denomination and that branch of the service. You can then be a second lieutenant in a reserve program. If you enter full time as a military chaplain, you enter as a captain. If serving as a military chaplain or a military reserve chaplain is of interest to you, contact the council of military chaplains of your denomination early in your seminary career.

It is pretty safe to say that the monetary and the retirement benefits for military chaplains will probably be superior to those of civilian clergy. Chaplains serve in the Army, Air Force, and Navy. (The Navy Chaplain Corps also covers the Marine Corps.) Each branch of the service has a different setup and emphasis when it comes to chaplains. Serving as a naval chaplain is different from serving as a chaplain in the Army or Air Force. You need to appreciate the differences. Let us conclude by returning to the words of Chaplain Hutcheson (p. 36): "Religious ministry never takes place in a 'spiritual' vacuum. It is always 'in' the world and 'for' the world. . . . The key to effective ministry as a military chaplain lies here: the secular institution must be understood; the form of ministry must be made relevant to the institution in which it is offered."

The Agony

The good news is that ordained ministers serve the church well in specialized ministries. The bad news is that specialized clergy often feel like outcasts. A professional minister who is called out of a local church to serve in an administrative capacity will often have people ask, "When did you leave the ministry?" It is like the time I asked a Methodist friend if he ever desired to become a bishop. His response was, "No, I prefer to stay in religious work."

Many feel that a clergyperson who is doing something other than preaching and administering the Sacraments is not really involved in ministry. W. K. Childress is Director of Pastoral Care at the Children's Hospital National Medical Center, Washington, D.C. As he describes his work, you be the judge if he really has a legitimate ministry:

> I frequently hold children as they die, remain with parents during the long hours of waiting outside an emergency or operating room, or play games with children whose parents are unavailable. By doing so, perhaps a chaplain lives out the words of the psalmist, "Yea though I walk through a valley as dark as death, I will not be afraid, because you are there with me."

Even though there is a movement afoot to be more supportive of people in non-parish settings and recognizing the special gifts which specialized clergy bring to bear on the lives of people, we are still a long way off. Even with this frustration, Frank K. McDowell looks toward retirement, grateful for the opportunity to be a pastoral counselor:

> I'm glad for the opportunities I have had, sorry for the ones I missed, but eternally grateful for being able to do what I read in the New Testament the Lord Jesus set out to do in his ministry. Namely, work with the outcast of society—the alcoholic, the obese, the neurotic, the lonely, the depressed, the angry, the bewildered, the hyperactive, the oversexed, the undersexed, the guilty, the fanatic, the defensive, the weak, the obnoxious, the passive, the white, the black, the brown, the genius, the retarded—you name it, I've worked with them, wept with them, prayed with them, and grown with them.

Many people who labor in specialized ministries are in settings other than stained-glass-window churches. John R. Thomas, a Navy chaplain and then a psychiatric chaplain, describes his parish setting by saying (p. 17), "My parish was a ship, or my pulpit was in the gymnasium of a psychiatric hospital, or my worship service was in a medical classroom." Although the setting and the emphasis may be a little different in specialized ministries, these professional ministers are still called to proclaim God's love in Jesus Christ to a hurting world. This often means being removed from polite society. George Bennett, former Dean of Students at Louisville Theological Seminary, talks about his former work as a chaplain in a psychiatric hospital and shares an experience about being in the "snake pit" (p. 36): "Once, in the 'snake pit'—the back ward of back wards of a state mental hospital—I was very, very nice to a very, very 'crude' patient She vomited on me."

Each particular call to ministry is unique. Every church that an ordained minister serves is different. Every call to a new position will be a new experience. This may include a call to a specialized ministry. If variety is the spice of life, the professional ministry is a spicy vocation. As has been stated from the beginning, we must be completely open to the way in which God might be leading us, and we need to be sensitive to the Spirit's force which prompts us to live out what we discover to be our unique call.

12

The Tight Job Market, or
A Call Is a Call

In the introduction of *Too Many Pastors?* (p. 17), there is a description of a cartoon that "pictures a young man wearing a clerical collar looking at a sign tacked to a Gothic-style church building. The sign reads, in bold letters: NO HELP WANTED!"

Within the mainline Protestant churches, we have achieved an interesting placement dilemma. Professional ministers are getting to feel like a dime a dozen in the marketplace.

Now before you get the wrong impression, note that this crisis is a very complicated one, with a large number of factors that bear on it. The situation, though, has some real implications for you, if you choose this vocation. In days gone by, denominational executives had to worry about how to supply all the vacant pulpits. Now the problem is how to place all the clergy looking for calls.

Reasons for the Clergy Surplus

In what follows, I rely heavily on an extensive study of placement by Jackson W. Carroll and Robert L. Wilson in their book *Too Many Pastors?* (to which the page numbers refer). For a closer examination of the subject, you will need to refer to their excellent research.

The percentage of individuals who have been trained to become professional ministers has increased over the past twenty years. However, the number of churches within the Protestant tradition has either not changed substantially or has decreased, over the same period of time (p. 38). As we saw in chapter 10, women have entered the job market recently and at the worst time since the 1930s depression (p. 77). If it were not for large numbers of women entering seminary, seminary enrollments would be down dramatically.

In these times, when a number of fields are crowded, the professional ministry may seem to be a better option than some other crowded field. I have interviewed many people who were considering either medicine or the ordained ministry. When the door to medicine was closed to them, they often opted for their second choice, the ordained ministry.

The local church employs the majority of professional ministers. When the church at large becomes inflated, a greater stress is put on how many are seeking employment in the local church. If professors trained to teach at a seminary are unable to obtain a position, they may move into the local church. This is true also for other specialists within the greater church. Thus the job situation can be rather fierce and, if I may be so nontheological as to say it, competitive.

Along with society in general, the church is also caught in a financial dilemma. Professional ministers are now generally paid better today than in the past, and the cost of health insurance and pension benefits continues to rise. The church facility must be heated, lights have to be lit, the roof kept in repair. In short, a full-time ordained minister may be too great an expense for a small congregation, when denominations require at least modest salaries for clergy. Even two or three small churches linked together, with a modern circuit rider, may find it difficult to support a professional minister. This is becoming even more critical in these times, when the denominations are less and less able to subsidize such ministries.

It is indeed ironic, when we consider the difficulty of placing ordained ministers in local churches, that there are a number of churches open and able to employ a professional minister that are having a difficult time trying to find an ordained minister to accept the call. These churches are normally small, in terms of membership, are often in small towns or in the country, and pay small salaries. This picture is backed up by the fact that the Plains States are not feeling the same clergy surplus as other parts of

71495

the country. For in the Plains States, there is a multitude of small isolated congregations.

The problem may be stated, as many people have done, that there is not a lack of pulpits to be filled by ordained ministers. The problem is that there are not the type and size of churches, in desirable geographic areas and paying respectable salaries, that ordained ministers are apparently seeking.

Mary V. Atkinson, who is in charge of placement in the Atlanta office of the Presbyterian Church (U.S.A.), wrote an article in *Presbyterian Survey* entitled "Too Many Ministers?" Her thought and research reveal that the problem is not an oversupply of clergy or an undersupply of churches, it is the desirable match that is creating problems. An example of this dilemma is pointed out by a survey of 100 average Presbyterian churches and 100 average ordained Presbyterian ministers and what each expects (p. 36).

- 55 of 100 churches prefer a person who is 54 years old or younger.
- 48 of the 100 churches would like their pastor to be married; only 2 were open to an unmarried minister.
- 40 of the 100 churches prefer a man for their pastor, with only one church in favor of having a woman pastor.
- 37 of the 100 churches prefer a person from the same racial or ethnic backround as the majority of the congregation, while only 3 preferred someone from a different racial or ethnic background.

It is obvious that what churches expect and what ordained ministers have to offer do not coincide very well statistically. Now let us take a look at what ordained Presbyterian ministers are seeking (p. 36):

- 50 would like to live in a suburban area or in a town, yet only 38 of 100 churches are in such settings.
- Many say they'd like a church in a college town or near a university, but there aren't enough churches so located to meet this preference for all who desire it.
- 2 prefer a church in a rural area, but more than 20 of 100 churches are rural.
- 1 prefers a church with fewer than 100 members, but 16 of the 100 churches are that size.
- 33 prefer churches within a membership range of 250 to 500, but only 17 of 100 churches fall into that range.

Seminary graduates seeking their first call are not the ones experiencing the greatest problem in the job market. Although the choices may be fewer than in the past, the average graduate will almost always get placed—unless the graduate is not open to moving or has too many personal restrictions. (Working spouses, of course, make this problem particularly acute.) "With the exception of the Episcopal Church most . . . denominations are not having serious difficulty placing new entrants. Although their choices are more limited, most new entrants are able to find jobs either on the staffs of large churches or as pastors of small churches." (Carroll and Wilson, p. 43.)

It is true that a large number of pastors will be retiring in the next decade, but it is difficult to say to what extent this will affect the job situation. It is possible that students entering seminary in the next several years will graduate into a much brighter job market. No one knows.

The problem of the abundance of clergy often becomes critical when a minister who has been out of school several years wishes to move. Movement may be difficult "upward," for lack of a better term. Seeking a new call may be a long, ego-smashing experience and trial. Many ordained ministers have been ingrained with the idea that success is measured by reaching the big-steeple church. When, at age forty, a minister realizes that he or she will probably never serve such a church, it becomes difficult. And when a minister gets ready to put his or her children through college, it may be virtually impossible on the salary offered by a small congregation. Also, in most instances, the older an ordained minister gets above the age of fifty, the less desirable that individual becomes in the marketplace.

Let us take a look at where the real job crunch is occurring. Denominations have various methods of placing clergy in local churches. It is possible to divide them into three types. Type A is a denomination, such as the United Methodist Church, where placement occurs on a guaranteed basis and the denominational officials assign clergy to churches. Type B, let us say, is at the opposite end of the placement system. This is a system, such as in the Southern Baptist tradition, where local churches have complete control over who they call to be their pastor, without outside interference. In between those two methods of deploying clergy, we have Type C. Presbyterian churches would be an example of this system, in which the congregation calls an individual to serve as the pastor; however, the denomination must also approve of the selection, and the individual must meet the requirements for ordination in that denomination.

The system having the greatest problem is Type C. Denominations whose clergy are experiencing difficulty in the job market include the Episcopal Church, the Presbyterian Church (U.S.A.), the Reformed Church in America, and the United Church of Christ. Technically, the United Church of Christ is a combination of Type B and Type C. According to Carroll and Wilson (p. 43), The United Methodist Church is experiencing some difficulty, and other denominations are experiencing a balance or a tight balance in the supply-and-demand relation of clergy to local churches. Only the evangelically oriented churches appear to be exempt from this concern because they are growing and beginning new congregations.

For those churches which are not assigned clergy, the whole placement system has become very sluggish. As many as one third of all ordained ministers in a given denomination may have active dossiers with very little movement going on. If a pastor cannot move, that pastor's present situation cannot open up for someone else. "One denominational executive compares the situation to an overcrowded expressway, where the sheer volume has reduced movement to a crawl. He comments, 'The entrance ramps are getting so crowded that it is even difficult to get on.' " (Quoted in Carroll and Wilson, p. 69.)

How This May Have an Impact
Upon Your Professional Ministry

If you begin your preparation for the professional ministry, you must know that there is a great likelihood that you will be entering a highly competitive field. It is also important to understand that the Master of Divinity degree is narrow in terms of its scope and will thus prepare you for little outside the realm of the church.

All this may mean that only those who are personally and professionally suited for the ordained ministry will survive. The difficult job market may put your "call" to the fullest test, once you have graduated from seminary. It is very possible, regardless of your qualifications, that you will never serve your ideal church, wherever that may be.

This whole picture may force you to examine a variety of ways in which you could fulfill your calling to the professional ministry. Tentmaking (where you work a second job to support yourself in the fashion of the apostle Paul), with all of its problems, may be an increasing option for clergy. The whole worker-priest concept may be revitalized.

Those who are more elastic in response to God's leading may be in a much better position. This is as true for women as it is for men, if not more so. After graduation from seminary, would you consider three small churches in the Nevada desert or a small congregation in a fishing village in Alaska? Or would you serve as an assistant pastor in a Detroit church or as the pastor of a rural church in the middle of Iowa?

One of the implications, already becoming a reality, is that ordained ministers may be staying longer in each church served. This means that you may be in one church for a long haul, as opposed to short-term relationships with several churches. You will have to face problems and deal with them, instead of moving on. After your abilities have been expended in the short-term ministry of three to five years, you will need to get serious about updating your skills and pursuing serious continuing education. Longer pastorates can be a mixed blessing, with both positive and negative factors.

Lyle E. Schaller, in his research (pp. 53–55), is convinced that one of the great stumbling blocks to church growth is short-term pastorates. "There is overwhelming persuasive evidence *from a long-term congregational* perspective [that] the most productive years of a pastorate seldom *begin* before the fourth or fifth or sixth year of a minister's tenure in that congregation." Thus, Schaller goes on to point out, the most productive years in the life of a congregation are often missed. It is just plain difficult to build a church with a lot of depth and enthusiasm if a congregation is switching pastors every three to five years.

The focus and the future of your ministry may be in learning how to develop a long-term ministry and long-term relationships. This may be especially true if you serve in a denomination which has an open means of deployment, as in Types B and C. This may also have some very beneficial effects on your spouse's employment and your family's being able to develop deeper roots.

There is a certain amount to be said for the itinerant concept of ministry, where a congregation is less centered around the pastor. However, with the costs of moving and the effects that short pastorates have had on congregations, even denominations that move their clergy on a regular basis are leaning toward slightly longer pastorates.

I cannot see the future, any more than you can, nor can I know what may or may not await you in the ordained ministry. However, be aware of the job situation in your denomination and learn how it operates. At the present time, that situation is a source of frustration for some pastors and a downright sore spot for others. This may be one peculiar way in which your call will be tested at various times in the course of your professional ministry.

Minority Placement

The church is in great need of minority professional ministers, with the one exception of Asians. "In general, the demand for trained minority ethnic leadership, whether black, native American (American Indian), or Hispanic, is greater than the supply" (Carroll and Wilson, p. 47). When the churches put out warnings about the job crisis for clergy, they always make clear that minority groups are the exception. These individuals are in great demand within the life of the church.

The real concern for our minority brothers and sisters who are interested in the ordained ministry lies in the familiar area of discrimination. We will gladly have "them" serve, but serve only in certain churches, in certain neighborhoods, and under certain conditions. As it is true for women, it has also been found to be true for minority pastors—the church is not always anxious to hire people without regard to sex, race, or national origin.

How to Prepare for an Inflated Job Market

Preparation is essential to enter a tough job market. You will need to make sure your qualifications are in good order. You will also need to attempt to come to grips with the possible restrictions on your future; restrictions you did not create and restrictions that ought not to destroy your ego.

Consider preparing for a creative ministry. If there is a need for Hispanic clergy, why not learn Spanish? Many churches go without pastors because of their need to have a bilingual one. There are a number of seminaries in the country that will help train you for a Spanish-American language ministry.

Youth Ministry and Christian Education specialists always appear to be in short supply within the church. Could you consider becoming a specialist in a particular area of the life of the church?

As I understand it, The Uniting Church in Australia is in short supply of pastors. The church apparently is willing to pay round-trip passage for professional ministers who are willing to serve for several years. If you have a little adventure in your soul, why not consider this option?

If tentmaking appears to be an arrangement you could live with, develop a compatible vocation. Learn how to make stained glass, drive a school bus, or prepare income tax returns.

How about doing something really radical? Consider becoming a small-church specialist. Interestingly, most seminary students appear to be recruited out of large churches in city settings. It is often a real shock for a seminary student to serve in a rural or small-town church. However, this is a real area of need. Why not intentionally prepare for a career in the small church? The model for ministry is a whole lot different from the large church you might presently be a member of.

You must know, from all those who came before you, that God has a very mysterious way of calling people to ministries that they certainly would have never imagined for themselves and yet have found significant beyond description.

The Meaning of Success

All people must wrestle with the meaning of success within their lives, and maybe clergy are especially perplexed by what it really means to be a success within the life of the church. As easy as it is to say that the amount of the paycheck, the size of the church, and the prestige associated with a given church do not really mean anything, ordained ministers may feel they do.

I am not so sure that clergy, any more than anyone else, can completely get away from the apparent need to be a success in earthly terms. However, we know that God has called us not to make a success of ourselves but to be faithful to our calling. It surely would be nice to have both, I suppose, but it just doesn't work out that way.

Loren B. Mead put it very well when he said (p. 145):

Most of us will work in ministries that will not look dramatic. Most of us will labor all our lives in congregations that are too small to be what the economists call "viable." Many of us will face conspicuous failures, if not at least quiet foul-ups. America in the next decade or two will need people unafraid to offer religious leadership in congregations and schools and communities. America and its churches will be living with frightening uncertainties, and will need people who are willing to give of themselves and to share their faith in the power of God. Those leaders are likely to live with a lot of trouble, and they may win no popularity contests and build no new cathedrals, but they are the kinds of leaders whom the people in churches have always wanted and needed.

Regardless of the tight job market, is it not a contradiction in terms to suggest that God has called too many people into leadership positions within the church? The oversupply of clergy may force the church into a deeper examination of ministry and provide some new and creative alternatives to the traditional ministry in the local church. Possibly the oversupply will help to provide a religious awakening. Whatever God has in mind, if our Master has called you to a particular task and to be part of his new scheme, then you really have little choice but to accept in faith God's call.

13

Your Call to Minister, or
The Journey Without an Ending

"The Lord said to Abram, 'Go from your country and your kindred . . . to the land that I will show you.'" At God's command, Abram packed up his belongings and his kinfolk and left. Where would we be if Abram, later Abraham, had not agreed to listen to God?

Moses was more of a problem to God. For in a day long ago, Moses was out keeping watch over his father-in-law's flock when suddenly a flame appeared in a bush. This bush was afire but it was not consumed, and out of that bush, God called out, "Moses, Moses!" Moses responded by saying, "Here am I." The Lord told Moses to take off his shoes because the ground upon which he stood was holy ground. Then Moses, standing in his bare feet, was commanded to lead the children of Israel out of Egypt. However, Moses was not anxious to do any such thing and kept mumbling something about being incompetent and a subscriber to the Peter Principle. God, though, could not be turned down.

God's promise to Moses is also true for us today. The Lord God reassured Moses with the powerful promise, "I will be with you." Where would our faith be if Moses had not led the children of Israel out of Egypt and to the Promised Land?

While Samuel was just a mere child in the temple, the Lord called out to him in the middle of the night, "Samuel! Samuel!" And Samuel said, "Speak, for thy servant hears." What if Samuel had refused to hear God?

The great prophet Isaiah was standing in the temple during a worship service when all of a sudden the earthly realm faded out and the heavenly realm faded in. God was seated high and lifted up, and heavenly beings chanted back and forth to one another, "Holy, holy, holy is the LORD of hosts; the whole earth is full of his glory." At the voice of God, the very foundations shook, and Isaiah utters, in the midst of this awesome vision, a confession of his unworthiness: "Woe is me! . . . for I am a man of unclean lips, and I dwell in the midst of a people of unclean lips." A seraphim flies over to Isaiah and touches his mouth with a burning coal which has been taken from the altar. Then, God asks, "Whom shall I send, and who will go for us?" Isaiah responds in faith with the simple words, "Here am I! Send me." What if Isaiah had said, "Send someone else"?

Jeremiah, another great prophet, was worried because he was young. Jeremiah says, "Ah, Lord GOD! Behold, I do not know how to speak, for I am only a youth." God equips Jeremiah for his task in this way, "Then the LORD put forth his hand and touched my mouth; and the LORD said to me, 'Behold, I have put my words in your mouth.'" What if Jeremiah had refused to utter the prophetic words which God put inside him?

Peter and Andrew, James and John, two sets of brothers in the fishing business, dropped their nets and left their boats when Jesus came by and simply said, "Follow me." What if these longshoremen had not been obedient to the Lord's call?

Matthew was sitting in the tax office when Jesus came by. Again, Jesus used those two words that cause people to leave their former ways and lives, "Follow me." What if Matthew had ignored the call of Jesus to be a disciple?

Saul, later to be known as Paul, had a dramatic experience with Jesus on the road that led to Damascus. After a bright light flashed from heaven, Paul was thrown to the ground and the risen Lord asked him, "Saul, Saul, why do you persecute me?" Soon afterward, Saul, the great persecutor of Jesus Christ, became baptized and was turned into the greatest missionary for Jesus Christ that the world has ever known. Where would we be if Paul had failed to heed the call of Christ to take the good news to the Gentiles?

It would be fascinating to speculate about "what if" with a lo of the biblical figures who were called by God. It would be fascinating to know what might have happened if someone failed to respond to the Lord's summons. However, this speculation is for nought, because when God has a task to be accomplished, our Lord has a tendency to offer calls one cannot refuse.

A call originates in God, and it must not be manipulated or distorted. At many times in the Gospel narratives, people came up to Jesus and wanted to follow him. The main problem with these people, such as with the rich young man, was that they wanted to follow Jesus on their own terms. When we follow Jesus Christ, we must be willing to follow on our Master's terms and not on our own. "You did not choose me," says Jesus, "but I chose you and appointed you that you should go and bear fruit and that your fruit should abide." God is referred to as the vinedresser and Jesus calls himself the vine. We are the branches, and apart from our Lord "can do nothing."

We have seen that the paramount call that God issues forth is a "call to be a Christian." Again, this is the foundational and the supreme call. Within this call, God will sometimes call individuals to a special task, which has been considered throughout this book. A call to a special office of leadership within the church is no more holy a call than the general call to be a Christian. Ordained ministers are not any holier than any other minister.

Throughout the biblical narrative, it is possible to see many people who did not receive a specific call but who did respond to the call to be faithful. God is dependent upon every person in every walk of life who dares to call upon the name of the Lord. A call to the ordained ministry is understood as a call to a specific function within the life of the church. It is not a call to join a spiritual hierarchy. A person who responds to a call to be a Christian is just as valuable and necessary in God's eyes as a person who responds to a call to a specific office. The importance is put not on where God has called us to serve but on our being obedient to God leading us.

It is really of little consequence whether you fulfill God's call through the ordained ministry or through the general ministry. What is important is that you respond in faith. You must know the radical claim which God has on your life, in order that you, like all ministers of the Lord, can live out the good news of Jesus Christ.

If you are still uncertain about where your call may be leading you, there is only one solution to your problem. You must live in obedience to the Master, who beckons you to pick up the cross of Christ. When you do, the answer is bound to become clearer to you. As the great German theologian Dietrich Bonhoeffer says in *The Cost of Discipleship* (p. 100), "But how is the Christian to know what kind of cross is meant for him? He will find out as soon as he begins to follow his Lord and to share His life." ("He" also means "she" in this instance.)

The first step always involves a great amount of risk. This risk could be translated as faith. As you attempt to live your life in the light of Jesus Christ, it is important to ask yourself, "What is the most important thing that I could do with my life to love God and to love others?" You must then wait upon the Lord for an answer.

God may have need of you to be a nurse or a social worker or an insurance agent or an ordained minister. Wherever life may lead you, you must know that the God we know in Christ beckons you to adhere to the two simple words of Jesus, "Follow me."

It is not important to know where God will lead you. It is important, though, to know that God in Christ is leading you. As Bonhoeffer put it (p. 41), "Only Jesus Christ, who bids us follow Him, knows the journey's end. But we do know that it will be a road of boundless mercy. Discipleship means joy."

Bibliography

Atkinson, Mary V. "Too Many Ministers?" *Presbyterian Survey,* Vol. 71, No. 3 (March 1981), pp. 36–37.

Bartlett, Laile. *The Vanishing Parson.* Beacon Press, 1971.

Bennett, George. *When They Ask for Bread; or, Pastoral Care and Counseling in Everyday Places.* John Knox Press, 1978.

Bernhard, Marianne. "Clergy Burnout: When Stress, Overwork Overwhelm the Spirit." *The Washington Post,* May 8, 1981.

Bonhoeffer, Dietrich. *The Cost of Discipleship.* Rev. ed., tr. by R. H. Fuller. Macmillan Publishing Company, 1963.

————. *Letters and Papers from Prison.* Ed. by Eberhard Bethge. London: Fontana Books, 1962.

Brightman, Lloyd, and Theodore A. Mollette. "The Impact of Seminary Experience on the Marital Relationship." *Journal of Pastoral Care,* Vol. XXXI, No. 1 (March 1977), pp. 56–60.

Calian, Carnegie Samuel. *Today's Pastor in Tomorrow's World.* Hawthorn Books, 1977.

Campbell, Donald. *Enlistment of Candidates in a Day of Job Scarcity.* Atlanta: The Office of Professional Development of the Presbyterian Church in the U.S.

Carroll, Jackson W., and Robert L. Wilson. *Too Many Pastors? The Clergy Job Market.* Pilgrim Press, 1980.

The Challenge to Be Presented in the Church's Program of Enlistment. New York: The Vocation Agency, Office of Counseling Resources, The United Presbyterian Church in the U.S.A., 1979.

The Chaplaincy Maybe Is for You. U.S. Government Printing Office, March 1, 1979.

Childress, W. K. "Pastoral Care in a Pediatric Hospital." *Monday Morning,* Vol. 46, No. 2 (Jan. 26, 1981), pp. 11–15.

Chilstrom, Herbert W. "The Pastoral Calling from the Perspective of a Bishop." *Word and World: Theology for Christian Ministry,* No. 1 (Fall 1981), pp. 331–337.

Coffin, William Sloane. *Once to Every Man: A Memoir.* Atheneum Publishers, 1978.

Daniel, Stephen, and Martha L. Rogers. "Burnout and the Pastorate." *Journal of Psychology and Theology,* Vol. 9, No. 3 (Fall 1981), pp. 232–249.

Erikson, Erik. *Young Man Luther.* W. W. Norton & Company, 1962.

Fairchild, Roy W. *Discerning Your Call and Your Gifts for Ministry.* New York: The Vocation Agency of The United Presbyterian Church in the U.S.A.

Glasse, James D. *Profession: Minister.* Abingdon Press, 1968.

Grider, Edgar M. *Can I Make It One More Year?* John Knox Press, 1980.

Hommes, Tjaard. "Authentic Ministry." *The Lutheran Quarterly,* Vol. XXIX, No. 1 (February 1977), pp. 58–65.

Hutcheson, Richard G., Jr. *The Churches and the Chaplaincy.* John Knox Press, 1975.

Jacobsen, David C. *The Positive Use of the Minister's Role.* Westminster Press, 1967.

Jacquet, Constant H., ed. *Yearbook of American and Canadian Churches, 1984.* Abingdon Press, 1984.

Jenkins, Daniel. *The Protestant Ministry.* Doubleday & Co., 1958.

Joint Report on Specialized Ministries. For the General Assemblies of The United Presbyterian Church U.S.A. and the Presbyterian Church in the U.S. New York and Atlanta: Offices of the Stated Clerks, 1981.

Jud, Gerald J., Edgar W. Mills, and Genevieve Walters Burch. *Ex-Pastors: Why Men Leave the Parish Ministry.* Pilgrim Press, 1970.

Kemper, Robert. *The New Shape of Ministry: Taking Accountability Seriously.* Abingdon Press, 1979.

Macdonald, Murdo Ewen. *The Call to Communicate.* Edinburgh: St. Andrew Press, 1975.

Mace, David and Vera. *What's Happening to Clergy Marriages?* Abingdon Press, 1980.

McCutcheon, James. *The Pastoral Ministry.* Abingdon Press, 1978.

McDowell, Frank K. "My Story of Specialized Ministry." *Monday Morning,* Vol. 46, No. 2 (Jan. 26, 1981), pp. 7–8.

Mead, Loren B. "Ministry's Subterranean Shifts. *Christian Century,* Vol. XCVIII, No. 4 (Feb. 4–11, 1981), pp. 141–145.

Model for Ministry: A Report for Study by the General Assembly Special Committee on the Theology of the Call. Ed. with an introduction and commentary by Lewis S. Mudge. New York: The United Presbyterian Church in the U.S.A., 1970.

Niebuhr, H. Richard. *The Purpose of the Church and Its Ministry: Reflections on the Aims of Theological Education.* In collaboration with Daniel Day Williams and James M. Gustafson. Harper & Brothers, 1956.

Niebuhr, Reinhold. *Leaves from the Notebook of a Tamed Cynic.* Shoe String Press, 1956.

Nouwen, Henri J. *The Wounded Healer: Ministry of Contemporary Society.* Image Books, 1979.

Oates, Wayne. *The Holy Spirit in Five Worlds: The Psychedelic, the Nonverbal, the Articulate, the New Morality, the Administrative.* Association Press, 1968.

Oswald, Roy M. *Crossing the Boundary: Between Seminary and Parish.* Alban Institute, 1980.

Perry, William E. *Orchestrating Your Career.* C.B.I. Publishing Company, 1981.

Presbyterian Panel Findings: The April 1980 Questionnaire. New York: The United Presbyterian Church in the U.S.A., April 1980.

Proctor, Priscilla and William. *Women in the Pulpit: Is God an Equal Opportunity Employer?* Doubleday & Co., 1976.

Rupert, Hoover. "Not What I Had in Mind." *Presbyterian Outlook,* Vol. 162, No. 7 (Feb. 18, 1980), p. 9.

Schaller, Lyle E. *Assimilating New Members.* Abingdon Press, 1978.

————, ed. *Women as Pastors.* Abingdon Press, 1982.

Schuller, David S., Merton P. Strommen, and Milo L. Brekke, eds. *Ministry in America: A Complete Report and Analysis Based on an In-depth Survey of 47 Denominations in the U.S. and Canada with Interpretation by 18 Experts.* Harper & Row, 1980.

Shedd, Charlie W. *Letters to Karen: On Keeping Love in Marriage.* Abingdon Press, 1965.

Statement on Preparation for Seminary Students. Vandalia, Ohio: The Association of Theological Schools, June 1978.

Switzer, David K. *Pastor, Preacher, Person: Developing a Pastoral Ministry in Depth.* Abingdon Press, 1979.

Thomas, John R. "Opportunity for Ministry in the Chaplaincy." *Monday Morning,* Vol. 46, No. 2 (Jan. 26, 1981), pp. 15–17.

Truman, Ruth. *An Underground Manual for Ministers' Wives.* Abingdon Press, 1974.

Walker, Jan C. *Why Me, Lord? The Mystery and the Reality of the Call.* C.S.S. Publishing Company, 1976.

Walters-Bugbee, Christopher. "Hard Pressed and Anxious: Seminaries Face the Eighties." *Christian Century,* Vol. XCVIII, No. 4 (Feb. 4–11, 1981), pp. 98–103.

Williams, Frank, "What Is Happening with Clergy?" *Symposium on the Future of Ministry* (cassette tape). Columbus, Ohio: Mid-West Career Development Center, 1978.